DIPLOMATIC MATERIAL

DIPLOMATIC MATERIAL

Affect, Assemblage, and Foreign Policy

JASON DITTMER

Duke University Press   Durham and London   2017

Typeset in Arno Pro by Westchester Publishing Services

Library of Congress Cataloging-in-Publication Data
Names: Dittmer, Jason, author.
Title: Diplomatic material : affect, assemblage, and foreign policy /
Jason Dittmer.
Description: Durham : Duke University Press, 2017. |
Includes bibliographical references and index. | Description
based on print version record and CIP data provided by
publisher; resource not viewed.
Identifiers:
LCCN 2017007584 (print)
LCCN 2017011337 (ebook)
ISBN 9780822372745 (ebook)
ISBN 9780822368823 (hardcover : alk. paper)
ISBN 9780822369110 (pbk. : alk. paper)
Subjects: LCSH: Diplomatic and consular service. | Diplomacy. |
Material culture. | Diplomatic and consular service—
Great Britain. | Material culture—Great Britain.
Classification: LCC JZ1405 (ebook) | LCC JZ1405.D58 2017 (print) |
DDC 327.2—dc23
LC record available at https://lccn.loc.gov/2017007584

Cover art (detail): Arnaldo Pomodoro, *Sphere within a Sphere*,
1963, diameter 120 cm., Hirshhorn Museum and Sculpture
Garden. © the artist. All rights reserved. Photo by Keith Stanley.

CONTENTS

For Florence, my sprout

BRUSA	Britain–United States of America circuit
CCM	Combined Cypher Machine
CFSP	Common Foreign and Security Policy
CIA	Central Intelligence Agency
CNAD	Committee of National Armament Directors
CSCE	Conference for Security and Cooperation in Europe
DSB	Defence Signals Branch
EC	European Community
ECHO	EU Directorate-General for European Civil Protection and Humanitarian Aid Operations
EEAS	European External Action Service
EPC	European Political Cooperation
EU	European Union
FCO	Foreign and Commonwealth Office
GC&CS	Government Code & Cipher School
GCHQ	Government Communications Headquarters
HUMINT	human intelligence
LSIB	London Signals Intelligence Board

MAS	Military Agency for Standardization
NSA	National Security Agency
NSO	NATO Standardization Office
OSCE	Organization for Security and Cooperation in Europe
OSINT	open source intelligence
PSC	Political and Security Committee
SIGINT	signals intelligence
STANAG	Standardization Agreement
UKUSA	United Kingdom–United States of America alliance
VTC	video teleconferencing
WEU	Western European Union

Doing this research and producing this volume has been easily the most exciting time of my academic career, largely because of the time I was able to spend immersing myself in the archives and meeting with national-security officials. This time was a luxury given to me as an Arts and Humanities Research Council Leadership Fellow (AH/K008110/1), for which I am immensely grateful. The fellowship not only freed me from teaching and administrative responsibilities but funded travel that was crucial to the completion of the project. I am also grateful to all my interviewees, as well as to the extremely helpful archivists at the National Archives (Kew), the NATO Archives, and the National Security Archive at George Washington University.

Central to the development of this project was my comrade-in-arms for all things diplomatic, Fiona McConnell, as well as the entire Diplomatic Cultures Research Network (AH/J013900/1). The experience of convening the research network was a baptism of fire for us in a new field; Fiona and I frequently commented to one another on how generous and accepting the scholars of diplomatic studies are. Perhaps the subject matter lends itself to such behavior. I am also grateful to the various audiences who helped me to hone my arguments, especially those at the University of Oxford, the University of Liverpool, the University of Glasgow, Uppsala University, University College London (UCL), the University of Cambridge (three times, no less), Harakopio University (three times as well), Newcastle University, Royal Holloway, the

University of Wisconsin, the University of Georgia, the University of North Carolina, the University of Colorado, Durham University, and several Association of American Geographers (AAG) conferences and pre-conferences. Two anonymous reviewers were key to the refinement of the written manuscript. Special thanks are due to Courtney Berger of Duke University Press, whom serendipity sat next to me at the 2015 Annual Meeting of the AAG. Her keen eye and support helped to bring the manuscript to completion. I would be remiss if I did not mention the staff at the Royal Standard pub in Blackheath, where an embarrassing amount of this book was written, as well as the good folks at Radio Margaritaville, who provided the soundtrack.

It goes without saying that no author does anything truly on his or her own. I am surrounded by colleagues at the UCL Department of Geography who make me a better teacher and scholar every day through their wide-ranging interests and intellectual rigor. The coincidence of my fellowship with the birth of our daughter meant that my wife, Stephanie, had to handle a lot all on her own while I was scampering off to Brussels or Washington or simply returning home late from Kew night after night. Her ongoing support for this project is something for which I am very grateful. Finally, I wish to thank all my family and friends. Every book project has its highs and lows, and this one has had more than most. I could not have done it without you all.

Geopolitical Assemblages
and Everyday Diplomacy

A scene from *A Tale of Two Cities* conveys Charles Dickens's wary view of mob violence during the French Revolution.

> Who gave them out, whence they last came, where they began, through what agency they crookedly quivered and jerked, scores at a time, over the heads of the crowd, like a kind of lightning, no eye in the throng could have told; but, muskets were being distributed—so were cartridges, powder, and ball, bars of iron and wood, knives, axes, pikes, every weapon that distracted ingenuity could discover or devise. People who could lay hold of nothing else, set themselves with bleeding hands to force stones and bricks out of their places in walls. Every pulse and heart in Saint Antoine was on high-fever strain and at high-fever heat. Every living creature there held life as of no account, and was demented with a passionate readiness to sacrifice it.[1]

We have all participated in scenes like this, if with lower stakes, such as a packed crowd at a rock concert. As part of the crowd we retain our sense of a rational self, observing the scene and making decisions, and yet we are also folded into an organized, though leaderless, collectivity. The materials at hand—here, muskets, bricks, and even the lives of the mob itself—are incorporated into the whirlpool of activity and shape its capabilities. Like a flock of birds turning in formation, the decision of the crowd is instantaneous and individual decisions are sublimated to it. To decide *not* to stampede is to be stampeded.

Geopolitical assemblages can form from nothing but the bodies of bystanders and a focal point for their attention. The intense affective atmosphere described by Dickens produces political subjects who might commit violence they would never otherwise consider committing. Not all geopolitical assemblages unfold in such a brief, local context. The same phenomenon was experienced by many in the spring of 2003, as the United States, Great Britain, and others from the "coalition of the willing" prepared for the invasion of Iraq. While a diplomatic solution was still formally on the table, many *felt* that the die had been already cast on both sides of the Atlantic, as indeed we later discovered it was.[2] Those who did so were being affected both by media flows carrying a pessimistic discourse from various governmental elites as well as by other directly sensed shifts: perhaps we saw soldiers who were being called up, or simply perceived a thirst for (displaced 9/11) vengeance in the air.[3] For those paying attention, the elements composing the state—diplomats, congressional resolutions, military equipment, citizens engaging in public discourse—were clearly aligned in a way that made war inevitable.

Or they at least made it seem that way. A similar atmosphere pervaded American public life almost exactly a decade later as the United States once again assembled a coalition to strike in the Middle East at a tyrant accused of using chemical weapons against his own people. This time however, it was Syria, and as the international coalition devoted to the rule of international law began to take shape, a similar pessimism took hold of many observers. Dickens's revolutionaries were stockpiling their bricks. However, when British Prime Minister David Cameron went to the House of Commons seeking authorization for British participation in the intervention, he was dealt a surprise defeat, the first time since 1956 that a prime minister had failed in such an effort. The reasons for the defeat were idiosyncratic and quite parochial—a combination of domestic partisanship and the hangover from the long intervention in Iraq. What was amazing was what happened next: deprived of its key military and diplomatic ally, the United States did a volte-face with regard to military intervention. The tension dissipated, and with the deflation of the affective intensity, new possibilities opened themselves up to the state apparatuses involved. A Russian offer to mediate between the United States and Syria was accepted, and soon thereafter the United States, Great Britain, and Syria were working together (in a manner of sorts) to defeat their common enemy, the Islamic State.

All three scenarios shared a few key elements. First, bodies were arranged in space and interacted with each other in an extradiscursive fashion, each caught up with the other in a form of collective agency. Both Dickens's crowd and the two "coalitions of the willing" were capable of much more than the individuals that compose them, but equally the collective decision-making was marked by an excess that cannot be reduced to rational thought. Second, the individuals involved—whether in the crowd or among the political elites—still perceived themselves to be individuals, even as their options (and subsequent decision-making) were shaped by the context in which they were operating. Finally, the result of the event could not have been predicted from the arrangement of the actors in space beforehand. In two cases it felt like violence was coming, and it was. In the third case it felt like violence was coming, but instead roles were scrambled and a completely unforeseen outcome emerged.

In this book I analyze the material circulations—of media, of objects, of bodies and their practices—that produce elite political subjectivities within the varying assemblages of the "international community" that has come into existence over the past few centuries. The history of the modern diplomatic system is marked by the rapid intensification of such flows, and yet relations between states continue to be conceptualized as the coming together of preexisting geopolitical subjects. I begin this volume with a rather different starting assumption: that the outside is always already inside the state apparatuses charged with "external" relations. The transnational circulation of these media, bodies, and practices brings affective potentials that subtly rework the political cognition of those engaged in foreign policy making.

This is not to advocate for the inclusion of the irrational in theories of foreign-policy formation; such arguments already exist.[4] Instead, I point to the more-than-rational, and indeed the more-than-human, nature of foreign policy. Rather than define the realm of diplomacy as the coming together of states, or even of their embodied representatives, I argue that the "international community" is the constant becoming-together of specific media, objects, and bodies/practices from which individual political subjectivities, states, and broader geopolitical communities (like "the West" or "Europe") emerge simultaneously.

Such an approach to foreign policy and international relations has two implications. First, it opens up key concepts that remain largely uninterrogated, such as "the national interest."[5] Rather than an elusive truth awaiting discovery by realist international relations scholars, or even the result of competing discursive communities (as might be argued by constructivists), the national interest is an emergent product not only of the political elites charged with formulating it but of the specific networks of transnational circulation in which those elites are already embedded. In short, the "we" of the national interest is always already *trans*national in some way. I trace the pathways in which this occurs within four unique case studies.

Second, and following from that point, my approach points to the importance of the microscaled and the baroque in specific foreign policies (such as the 2003 invasion of Iraq), and even in the emergence of alliances and other long-standing institutional arrangements. This is in contradiction to the predominantly macroscaled way in which these issues are typically framed, such as through structural forces or historical trends. A microscaled analysis of state foreign-policy apparatuses is particularly useful because those apparatuses are enmeshed in multiple alliances and arrangements, and are consequently buffeted by affective forces simultaneously. Therefore, in this volume I not only elaborate each chapter as a stand-alone case study, but also conclude by reading them against each other to assess their mutual interactions.

Still, we are at the beginning and not the end. In the remainder of this introductory chapter I elaborate my theoretical framework: one that builds up from local contexts and situations such as those described by Dickens and yet speaks to the broader world of international relations. Following that, I turn to the research design that underpins this book and its structure, followed by details of the methods deployed in each case study.

Affect, Assemblages, and International Relations
The New Statecraft

In this section I productively pull together the scholarship on the politics of everyday life with the political theory of the state. Rather than seeing these two literatures as opposed to one another in a narrow dispute over where politics is to be found, I argue that recent trends in both enable a fruitful connection. The literature on the politics of everyday life has foregrounded the importance of practices, habits, and bodies in the dynamic politics of the workplace and home (see, for instance, the conceptual emergence of microaggression).[6] These concepts are mirrored in a humanities-inflected literature on state theory that emphasizes the everyday coproduction of state effects and affects, and therefore the insights derived from the literature on the politics of everyday life can be conceptually brought to bear on the microscaled politics of the state, its bureaucracies, and the experiences of those who interact with those bureaucracies. Because these humanities-inflected approaches to the state tend to downplay the agency of materials, I also incorporate insights from science and technology studies and related fields.

Recent years have seen political geographers avoid the topic of the state—the traditional subject matter of the subdiscipline—in favor of a wider definition of the political that emphasizes everyday practices. This was first inspired by the adoption of the philosophy of Michel Foucault as the basis for a wide swath of political geography research; his emphasis on power as diffuse and relational has proven enduring within the field.[7] This approach to power and politics has been taken in new and unexpected directions, with scholarship focusing on bodies and everyday practices coming from scholars inspired by feminist approaches and popular geopolitics (or both).[8] Collectively, these investigations have highlighted the interplay between activities long imagined as occurring at different scales. Rather than a scalar imagination that privileges the global over the national or the local, we are presented with a world in which microscaled practices (such as domestic life, working practices, and so on) often defy the macroscaled narratives and structures that we imagine to be governing social life.[9] "This is the theoretical opportunity then: to investigate not the large systems but the small, the irregular, and the baroque."[10] This has entailed not a turn to the minor or the obscure, but a recognition of the translocal nature of social phenomena. Larger scales are not simply the aggregate of various locals; they are emergent from the enmeshing and interaction of various local events and phenomena.

A parallel maneuver in political theory has called into question the nature of the state itself. Drawing on Foucault's work on disciplinary power, these scholars have posited that the state does not exist as such, but is an emergent effect of a range of practices occurring at a range of sites.[11] For instance, the agency of the state emerges from governmental technologies and practices such as border management, taxation, census taking, market regulation, and birth, death, and marriage registration.

These banal bureaucratic endeavors underpin the seeming timelessness of the state, enabling it to cohere through time and to act. Nevertheless, the actual bureaucratic processes themselves vary extensively over time, and some of them are fairly recent additions to the ensemble of state activities. Therefore, the state appears to be a transcendental subject that orders the political world, when in reality it is the effect of that political world. The shift from examining the state itself to examining state effects in the realm of political theory is a clear parallel to developments in theoretical geography, although the latter have tended to be couched in terms of scales rather than of states.[12]

By putting these literatures in dialogue, I hope to cut a Gordian knot that has bedeviled political geography over the past twenty years. During that time, the state came to be seen as a stunted site of the political: a trap from which progressive scholarship must escape in order to understand the everyday violence of race and gender, to imagine alternative configurations of power, and to avoid capture by statist impulses toward imperialism and oppression. In disavowing the state so completely, however, political geography perpetuated a political binary—one could study state politics, or one could study everyday politics, but not both. Worse, there was the subtle implication that studying the state was politically naïve.

I am not alone in the effort to rehabilitate the state within political geography. A literature has emerged which I term "the New Statecraft," as it is principally concerned with the everyday crafting of the state. This work has taken inspiration primarily from the humanities. Joe Painter, for instance, turned to the concept of prosaics, as derived from Mikhail Bakhtin's literary theory: "Prosaics highlights the intrinsic heterogeneity and openness of social life and its 'many-voiced' character. It challenges all authoritative monological master subjects (God, Man, the Unconscious, the Sovereign as well as the State) and their efforts to impose authoritative meanings."[13] This approach valorizes the mundane encounters with statist discourse that constitute our everyday lives, such as election posters, policy papers, political speeches, road signs, and so on. However, this field of discourse is always polyvocal and therefore open to a range of affective, more-than-rational forces that undercut the state's claim to transcendent timelessness. The prosaic state is constantly becoming otherwise, as creative expressions constantly challenge its finalizability.

One implication of thinking through state effects rather than states is that it opens up the state-nonstate divide in highly productive ways.

Instead of ruling certain states "in" and other polities "out," we can begin to think of *all* polities as exhibiting certain qualities associated with stateness, while lacking others. Indeed, as the prosaic state illustrates, the legitimacy of even "obvious" states such as the United Kingdom relies on everyday encounters with the state to maintain the desired effect. But the concept of the prosaic state is not the only one to incorporate literary theory to state theory; Homi K. Bhabha's concept of mimicry has been taken up by scholars considering the diplomatic performances of polities struggling to achieve international legitimacy.[14] Bhabha notes that while colonial projects aim to produce modern subjectivities within the colonized, they do so within a field of power relations that relies on the construction of inalienable difference between colonizers and colonized. While colonizers officially claim to be "civilizing" the colonized, the legitimacy of the colonial intervention itself relies on a "proliferation of inappropriate objects that ensure its strategic failure, so that mimicry is both resemblance and menace."[15] In other words, mimicry of the colonizer's culture—in this case, the performance of diplomacy—ensconces the European state as an ideal to which others should aspire; however, if the diplomacy of the "illegitimate" polity is too good it may "pass" for a "real" state, showing how permeable the category really is (or might be).[16]

If diplomatic practices are transmuted into texts to render them subject to literary theory, they are somewhat robbed of their creative political potential. Another humanities-inflected approach draws on the theatrical and musical language of improvisation to remedy this reductionism. Pierre Bourdieu's concept of virtuosity identifies the ways in which actors improvise on social scripts.[17] Alex Jeffrey defines improvisation as "performed resourcefulness," asserting the centrality of embodied practice within "a context of limited possibilities."[18] That is, state elites (and those who would wish to be state elites) draw on a repertoire of discursive and material resources in their improvised performances of stateness. A multiplicity of state projects may be simultaneously performed by various actors in the same territory, each trying to deploy various state institutions, heritages, and infrastructures to their own advantage.

The abbreviated temporality of embodied performance vis-à-vis the literary text, however, begs the question of how the state appears to cohere over time in this formulation of statecraft. This question is frequently answered with reference to symbolic capital, the state's accumulation of legitimacy, which imbues its performance with an authority that others tend to lack.[19] This assumption—as well as Bourdieu's larger body of work on habitus, the embodied predispositions that accumulate over time within specific fields of practice—permeates the work characterized as the "practice turn" in international affairs and diplomatic studies, and has advanced thinking in those fields immeasurably.[20] Collectively, symbolic capital and habitus can be understood as some of the key resources from which diplomats and policy makers can draw in their efforts to improvise the state over time.[21]

But missing from these accounts is any notion of materiality *beyond* the body and its habituation. The introduction of new objects and materials to a habitus opens up new potentials—often unexpected—while also providing a new surface into which the state's symbolic capital can be inscribed. Therefore, while the valuable contribution of these humanities-based metaphors must be acknowledged, additional inspiration must be taken from philosophers of science.

The rise of more-than-human philosophy in political geography and international relations in recent years has pushed political scholars to pluralize both the forms of politics in need of address and our notions of agency within those politics.[22] This emphasis on pluralizing is important, as an emphasis on objects is not meant to displace the insights of humanities-inflected approaches; rather, the state is the emergent effect of an assemblage of discourses, performances, and objects that act back on "us" as political subjects.[23] It is the latter element—objects—that the philosophy of science offers to political theory. Some impute an essential power to objects in and of themselves, what Jane Bennett has referred to as "vibrant matter."[24]

Central to the thrust of this work has been a shift in the metaphysics of the state, with the more plural notion of "force relations" dethroning "social relations" as the field from which state effects emerge.[25] Such an approach emphasizes the ways in which human subjects both position themselves and are positioned by their locus within these assemblages.[26] Indeed, it is the world of objects that paradoxically outlines the boundary of the human.[27]

The shift in emphasis to force relations is in part a shift to affect, the elusive relation of power inherent to the material world: "State power is therefore located in the interaction or *passage* between objects, implicated fully in *what* extensive alliances are assembled, and *how* these alliances are assembled (which affects are brought to the surface of an object, and which are left behind)."[28] Indeed, alongside the transcendent-seeming quality of state effects, we must attend to the constitutive power of state *affects* in composing the state as a geopolitical subject with agency.[29] It is in the slippages between what the state is supposed to be and what elements are composing it in any situated moment that instances of rupture can be exploited by those seeking to erode state effects, if only fleetingly.

I have taken developments in everyday politics and in state theory and productively brought them together to displace the notion of a coherent state in favor of a metaphysics of state effects and state affects, themselves the results of improvised practices by state elites and others. In the next section I go a step further, conceptualizing the world of states as a relational space composed of discursive and material flows that act back on the state apparatuses nominally composing the space. Agency, in this model, can be found not only in the states but also in the wider realm of force relations.

Sociomateriality, Diplomacy, and Transnational Affects

Having incorporated materiality and objects into my account of state effects, it is incumbent now to frame them conceptually. In this section I first outline the basics of assemblage theory, emphasizing how it adopts a flat ontology that emphasizes openness, dynamism, and self-organization. These qualities make assemblage a fascinating lens through which to consider both the state and the diplomatic system in which it is always already embedded. I do so through the notion of the body politic, which emphasizes the synchronic emergence of political subjectivities at multiple scales. It is my application of the body politic concept to diplomatic theory that enables a reconceptualization of the international community (in all its variants) as a series of material relations between state apparatuses: a political agency that is emergent both *through* and *above* the state. This agency has been woefully underexamined in the literature until now, as have the technologies (such as protocols) enabling it to emerge in the particular form we see today. I will now articulate my argument in more detail.

Assemblage theory has washed across human geography and to a lesser extent international relations, refreshingly without a conceptual monoculture taking root. Assemblages are understood to have five common characteristics.[30] First, assemblages are formed through relations of exteriority among constituent elements, and therefore the elements cannot be reduced to their function within the assemblage.[31] The characteristics of the assemblage cannot be assumed from the properties of the constituent elements; it is the capacities of the constituent elements when brought into relation with one another that matter.

Second, assemblages are productive of novelty. They are constantly becoming otherwise as elements come and go, and as elements "within" the assemblage *that are also assemblages in their own right* go through their own processes of becoming otherwise. While assemblages may seem to cohere in certain forms over time, this is more a function of the spatial and temporal scale at which they are being observed than it is a statement of the assemblage's own persistence.

Third, assemblages are, by definition, composed of heterogeneous elements. As Manuel DeLanda highlights, "The components of social assemblages playing a material role vary widely, but at the very least involve a set of human bodies properly oriented (physically or psychologically) towards each other."[32] Therefore, while social assemblages likely include a discursive component, they cannot be *purely* discursive.

Fourth, assemblages are impossible to authoritatively delimit. Because they are open systems, with elements constantly entering and leaving, the only possibility is to attempt to describe trends in their relational space over time. The terms *territorialization* and *deterritorialization* refer to processes by which an assemblage becomes, respectively, more or less coherent and delineated. Similarly, processes of coding and decoding designate the processes by which meaning is ascribed to assemblages or by which they become less laden with meaning—this meaning could be discursive or otherwise (e.g., the coding of living cells by DNA).

Fifth, assemblages are marked by desire. While this might imply an anthropomorphic dimension, desire instead refers to what Nietzsche described as the "will to power," that is, "a (nonpsychical, impersonal) will or impetus to more, to the increase of power, to the enhancement, not of a self or its ability to survive, but of its own forces, its own activities."[33] Put differently, this desire is the potential in every system for self-organization that can produce new things, new life, and new ways of being in the world.

How might assemblage thinking be used to reenvision states and their diplomatic relations? After a long functionalist history of considering the state as a "body politic," recent scholarship has infused the term with an assemblage sensibility.[34] In this formulation, bodies politic include any assemblage in which human bodies participate (akin to De-Landa's "social assemblages") and which shape the political cognition of those participating in them.[35] These can be short-lived and seemingly divorced from the politics of states (such as Dickens's mob) or they can be a traditional institution or apparatus (such as a university or the state itself). It is notable that in this conception the state is not special; it is simply one body politic among many.

There is a heuristic divide between first- and second-order bodies politic. First-order bodies politic are individual human subjects, whose bodies are themselves assemblages that shape perception of the social categories through which difference is understood, and that rely on various material flows, such as media, food, water, and so on. Second-order bodies politic include any assemblage in which multiple humans participate, such that there is some degree of collective affective cognition. These, too, depend on material flows, and they have their own metabolisms that stave off dissolution. Crucially, first-order bodies politic are not prior to second-order bodies politic, as in social-contract theory or liberal theories of the state. Rather, first- and second-order bodies politic are mutually engaged in processes of becoming together in synchronic emergence.

When this concept of bodies politic is laid alongside traditional notions of diplomacy, it both speaks to traditional concerns (relations between states, as materialized in both the building of permanent embassies and the embodied exchange of ambassadors) and yet also points to new possibilities. It shifts attention away from *states* as bodies politic (the usual stance within international relations) toward the *diplomatic system* itself as a type of body politic, the existence of which shapes the first- and second-order bodies politic embedded within it.[36] There is congruence here with Foucauldian approaches to governmentality, or the conduct of conduct. For instance, it has been noted that it was the experience of the foreign by early diplomats that produced them as ideal subjects of the sovereign: their posting to a foreign capital rendered them absolutely loyal to their master.[37] In other words, participation in the diplomatic assemblage shaped the subjectivities of civil servants in similar ways, even if the specific loyalty varied.

However, the individual's loyalties were rarely singular. Just as elements of an assemblage can participate in multiple assemblages at once, early ambassadors rarely served only one master; while overseas representing their sovereign, they frequently also represented their religious or local communities as well.[38] Nevertheless, as the state grew in political hegemony and colonized the spaces of diplomacy, narratives of alter-diplomacies were marginalized and are only now starting to return.[39] It is thus clear that in the early modern period diplomacy occurred through states, but was nevertheless more multifarious than that; diplomacy entailed the synchronic emergence of multiple bodies politic at once, often through the diplomacy of a single ambassador (also a body politic in his or her own right).

Stuart Elden traces this phenomenon at the negotiation of the Treaties of Westphalia, in which both the modern state and the diplomatico-military *dispositif* of Europe can be seen as becoming together.

> War is intended to be used judiciously, with a clear sense of why it is being fought, and used strategically to reinforce the balance of power. Diplomacy is to become an instrument or tool, with the negotiations in Westphalia as a model, with a congress of all states involved, and with a system of permanent ambassadors. Europe is seen as a juridico-political entity in itself, with a system of diplomatic and political security; but this is underpinned by the third instrument, each state having a permanent military apparatus of professional soldiers with an infrastructure of fortresses and transport, and sustained tactical reflection.[40]

From this it can be seen that bodies politic form at scales "above" the state (e.g., Europe), but often do so *through* the objects and practices of the state. Further, an assemblage approach to diplomacy likewise highlights a feature of early modern diplomacy that has often been eclipsed. Rather than being the opposite of war, diplomacy is one aspect of a larger dispositif, including the military, which worked to regulate the metabolisms of Europe. Thus, my concern in this volume with military diplomacy and signals intelligence can be seen as a throwback to earlier understandings of diplomacy rather than as yet another expansion of the field.

Given all this, it is clear that diplomats are multivalent—even in this age in which diplomacy is largely viewed as a state enterprise meant to enact the national interest. Indeed, it is precisely the doubleness of diplomatic practices—simultaneously of the state and yet beyond it—that has the potential to reshape the national interest. If today's diplomats frequently gain legitimacy from their state credentials and are therefore expected to represent the national interest, elite diplomats craft an identity that is somewhere in-between, repositioning both their government position and their interlocutors in order to get a positive result.[41] It is for this reason that foreign ministries are often viewed askance by elected officials and other civil servants. Foucault defines *milieu* as the space in which affective circulations occur, as the "intersection between a multiplicity of living individuals working and coexisting with each other in a set of material elements that act on them and on which they act in turn."[42] It is diplomats' very situatedness within a nonnational milieu that enables the channeling of affects from beyond the state assemblage into the very heart of power. Their bodies are yet one more variable in the "government of things" that needs to be managed by state authorities, for instance by rotating time in the capital with time overseas (a "tour" in a foreign posting is commonly three years, and a diplomat is unlikely to return to that post in their career).[43] At an even more microscale, diplomats' bodies as well as geographically resonant ingredients, dinnerware, and seating cards must be carefully managed in diplomatic sites—such as Iver Neumann's example of a state dinner—if the desired result is to be achieved.[44]

However, traditional diplomacy is only one avenue through which elements of state assemblages are brought into relation. Assemblage theory directs our attention to the wide array of sites and objects that can become enrolled in the transnational body politic formed by state assemblages.[45] The web of relations connecting these sites and objects is perhaps less glamorous than that of traditional diplomacy, but is arguably a much more intensive set of material connections. For instance, the latest round of globalization has seen the intensification and acceleration of various flows, from digital data to more traditional transportation and shipping. These are not just "content" or "goods," but also vectors for affect that can ripple through first- and second-order bodies politic, reshaping political cognition. The breathtaking expansion of these flows has had the effect of ruining the monopoly of foreign ministries on the foreign, with ministries of defense, finance, justice, and environment all taking on diplomatic roles.[46]

This increased connectivity between state apparatuses relies on the harmonization of the technical practices of governmentality.[47] This harmonization has been ongoing for a long time; among the oldest examples is diplomatic protocol itself, which provides an interface between state assemblages.[48] This interface dates back to the humorously named "Protocol on Protocol," incorporated in 1815 at the Congress of

Vienna, which was intended to provide a set of rules to avoid international conflicts over aristocratic honor and precedence. The concept of protocol is carried through all of the diplomacies of this volume's case studies. Some protocols are embodied routines and dispositions (as is diplomatic protocol), and some take the form of nonhuman objects that mediate affects. Other forms of harmonization are as contemporary as the technologies that prompt them, such as Internet protocols, the United Nations Convention on the Law of the Sea, and extradition treaties. Each protocol provides a means to extend a transnational governmentality across space that both expands the state's ability to act but also renders it subject to heightened flows of affect.

It would be easy to portray this process of harmonization as an inexorable flattening of difference, and narratives of globalization have often portrayed it as such. However, as assemblage theory indicates, it is not possible to assume the result of an interaction from the properties of the elements brought into relation. Therefore, the different protocols utilized in different processes result in unique relationships with difference, and therefore in different spatialities of power. These spatialities are the result of the specific histories of assemblage in each case, although those histories are not determinative of futures; rather, they are resources that can be drawn on in the various political actors' open-ended improvisations.

Flat(ter) Ontology, Scale, and Power

In this section, I articulate the high stakes of my theoretical framework. I begin by noting that traditional approaches to international relations have generally failed to predict major events; while an assemblage-influenced approach might not prove any better at prediction, it does at least explain why so many surprises await international relations analysts. The stakes are higher than the credibility of academic analysts, however. Attempts to account for the affective power of these geopolitical assemblages have often resorted to macroscaled theories of civilizational conflict or affinity that themselves reinforce already extant racist or xenophobic discourses (as in, most famously, the Clash of Civilizations thesis), with real-world consequences for those caught up in today's refugee crises and drone strikes. These discourses cannot be countered with mere deconstruction, but require constructive accounts that explain the actual empirical phenomena in question. I therefore offer a microscaled account of power, using Bruno Latour's concepts of *puissance* and *pouvoir*, which helps us to understand the evolution of geopolitical assemblages over time. As I hope will be clear, the theoretical and political implications of this approach are weighty.

The rise of assemblage thought in the social sciences has not been without its critics. For some, the use of assemblage simply overcomplicates social processes, or culminates in a thick description of a phenomenon.[49] For others assemblage is a distraction from the "real" leftist project of political economy.[50] For yet others, the debate lies in the nuances of various relational, materialist theories such as DeLandan assemblage or Latourian actor-network theory.[51] Its uptake in the world of international relations has been rather slower than in other fields, but nevertheless a strong toehold has been gained.[52] It shares with the Bourdieu-inspired work of the practice turn a disdain for the individualism of rational-choice theory, the determinism of Marxism, and the binary of structure-agency. Bourdieu's concept of the field superficially resembles the assemblage, but crucially the field is shaped by *social* relations rather than *force* relations.[53] The inclusion of the nonhuman in assemblages distributes agency through the field in a way that Bourdieu could not foresee. However, I am not arguing for a new hegemony of assemblage thought in international relations, diplomatic studies, or political geography. Assemblage theory can happily coexist with other schools of thought. However, assemblage thought is useful in highlighting the diversity of human and nonhuman actors implicated in any political moment, in inspiring us to think differently about classic topics, and in providing a conceptual language that speaks to a more-than-human world where change—of regimes, of technologies, of climate—is constant.

The inability of the discipline of international relations to anticipate macroevents such as the collapse of the Soviet Union, the War on Terror, and the Arab Spring has been well documented. Of course, "knowing the future" is a high standard to which to hold any discipline. However, given that international relations privileges systemic-level analysis and the continued belief in "law-like regularities," this failure should lead to a reconsideration of the discipline's theoretical bases.[54] Of course, the constancy of surprise is a strong indicator of the nonlinear outcomes one expects from assemblages exhibiting complexity.

Indeed, a belief in reductionist models of the political has bedeviled the social sciences for a long time, but this is particularly manifest when considering the politics of states, which are tremendously complex bodies politic and yet have often been reduced to billiard balls in space or other simplistic models.[55] By assuming the state as the foundation of "actorness" in international affairs, these models ignore the collective agency that forms when these bodies politic are linked together in an assemblage of circulating materialities and affects. This results in an inability to account for the empirical evidence of this collective agency, which like a poltergeist can be seen to be acting back on its constituent parts: states, their foreign-policy apparatuses, and the buildings and people that compose them.

One such attempt to explain away the collective agency of assemblages is civilizational thinking. While the idea of civilizations has a long and complex genealogy, there has been a resurgence of interest— sometimes critical, sometimes not—in the topic among scholars of international relations in the last two decades, fueled by both the War on Terror and the rise of China.[56] The renaissance of civilizational thinking at the turn of the millennium is of course diverse, including a divide between substantialist approaches (in which civilizations simply *are*) and processual or relational approaches (which see civilizations as the result of various geopolitical projects).[57]

Of course, the fact that substantialist authors feel compelled to argue their case implies that, in truth, all civilizations are embedded in discourse. Indeed, the rise and fall of civilizations in recent times can be seen to result not from imperial decadence or crop failure, but from changing discursive fashions. For instance, "the West" became popular during the Cold War in opposition to "the East" of the Soviet Bloc.[58] The uncomfortable merging of the West with the primarily religious civilizational essences invoked by Samuel P. Huntington might have led to the obscurity of his theory on the clash of civilizations were it not for the 11 September 2001 attacks, which seemed to give his ideas basis in fact. This boost for the idea of the West lasted but a short while, as the clash-of-civilizations thesis undercut the George W. Bush administration's attempts to build a coalition against Al Qaeda that incorporated non-Western countries.

Alongside the West—never fully replacing it—another civilization has taken form: the Anglosphere. Like the West, the Anglosphere is not a new idea; rather it is a resurrection of racialized colonial terms such as *white dominions* and *Anglo-Saxon world*. After World War II there were many attempts to preserve the wartime alliance between the United States and United Kingdom, and proponents often invoked the linguistic and broader cultural relations between the two.[59] More recently the historian Robert Conquest and the businessman James C. Bennett have argued for a notion of the Anglosphere that draws energy from the Internet and its network ontology.[60] They argue that this has intensified a sense of collectivity among English speakers around the world, who can now communicate with each other more easily than ever. They even include English-speaking groups in otherwise non-Anglophone countries, although the core of the Anglosphere is the "special relationship" between the United States and the United Kingdom. Indeed, a statistical analysis of U.S.-led military interventions in the second half of the twentieth century discovered a strong correlation between the English language and participation in American coalitions: "When push comes to shove, the English-speaking peoples tend to flock together."[61] How to make sense of this empirical phenomenon?

Advocates for the Anglosphere argue that culture is a homogenizing force, productive of commonality. In the case of the Anglosphere, the drive toward commonality has been largely progressive, with the British hegemony of the 1800s seen as ending the slave trade, and the American hegemony of the 1900s seen as ending the twin totalitarianisms of Nazism and communism. Thus, the Anglosphere of the 2000s can end "singularity, or the habit that states have of acting alone."[62] The progressive globalist framing of the Anglosphere clearly connects this "civilization" to whiteness and other cultural drivers.[63] Here and elsewhere, culture can be seen as a reductionist mode of analysis that flattens out difference into "singularity" to explain macroscaled geopolitical patterns.[64]

Civilizational thinking is just one iteration of a general problem in the analysis of international affairs: a desire to locate power in a scalar hierarchy in which "the global" or "the national" dominates "the local." Rather than a push toward singularity or the macro, an assemblage analysis highlights the importance of the heterogeneous and the micro. The indeterminacy of assemblage processes means that the macro is not simply the aggregation of the micro, but instead the effect of a range of elements—understood as existing in a flat ontology rather than a scalar imagination—that have come together in unique, historically contingent ways. Even seemingly timeless macro concepts such as the "national interest" which are understood to structure international relations are in truth multiplicitous and far from straightforward. "Political economies and structures emerge as relational products assembled through multiple routes, actors, histories, contingencies, resources, socio-materialities and power relations."[65] In short, the national interest is hardly something dictated by physical geography or economic necessity; it becomes materialized through a series of assemblages (think tanks, political parties, universities, embassies, lobbying groups, media networks, and so on) interacting with one another and coalescing (for a time) around a certain set of policy documents. As has been seen many times over, unexpected circumstances or a change of government can lead to a reshuffling of these assemblages, with a new national interest emerging from their interaction.

A central argument in this volume is that when foreign-policy apparatuses of the state enter into assemblage with one another, whether through traditional diplomacy or in more bureaucratic encounters associated with the international relations of the late twentieth century, they open themselves up to transnational affects that rework the basis on which national interest is calculated. So why would states do this? I answer this via Latour's twin concepts of power, *pouvoir* and *puissance*. States (or more accurately, elites within state assemblages) enter into assemblage with each other in order to enact their collective agency as actualized power (pouvoir, a "concrete ensemble of relations"), to increase their own capabilities (or sense thereof).[66] This necessarily opens them up to the immanent power to affect and be affected (puissance), from which state elites attempt to insulate the state apparatus through techniques such as rotating diplomats between the capital and overseas. Nevertheless, the excess of puissance means that attempts to tame these transnational affects will always be at best partially successful. In other cases, such as the foundation after World War II of what is now the European Union (EU), the whole point of entering into assemblage is to rework state assemblages through technical means rather than traditional political ones, thus initially privileging puissance over pouvoir.

One criticism of assemblage theory has been that its flat ontology was equally flattening of power relations. In the abstract this is true; without a scalar imagination on which to prop up an a priori understanding of power and its location, power is simultaneously everywhere and nowhere. However, on empirical examination of a particular assemblage, the flux of power in particular spaces and times is usually perceptible, if perhaps only afterward. "Part of the appeal of assemblage, it would seem, lies in its reading of power as multiple co-existences—assemblage connotes not a central governing power, nor a power distributed equally, but *power as plurality in transformation*."[67] Therefore, the flat ontology of assemblage is perhaps better understood as merely flatter than most; the constant becoming of the assemblage means that in certain times and spaces some elements of the assemblage will matter more than others, but in another configuration or constellation their importance will recede. The perception of this flux and flow is a matter of research method and researcher sensibility.

Research Design

In this book I attempt to trace geopolitical assemblages, such as civilizations or "the international community," that emerge "above"—and through—the state, with the purpose of producing an account of the collective agency that is attuned to the microscale of practices and objects rather than resorting to the reductionism of macroscale structures. I offer a counterhistory of British foreign-policy making in which the focus is not on what the British state decided to do "in the world," but rather on how "the world" was already *inside* those policy-making processes as a result of Britain's historic leading role in forging geopolitical assemblages. The structure of this book reflects my desire to juxtapose a range of dimensions of foreign policy (diplomacy, intelligence, and defense) as well as a range of transnational assemblages, some of which are bureaucratic organizations and some of which are not. As Martin Müller argues, "Following traces, collecting evidence and charting who connects with whom and through what does not mean that analysis must remain within the boundaries of one particular organization."[68]

I begin with a case study of the nineteenth-century British Foreign Office and its relations with paper and other materialities, through which British foreign policy was created and enacted around the world. I then turn to intelligence cooperation between the United Kingdom and the United States during World War II, which over time emerges as the UKUSA (or "Five Eyes") alliance in which signals intelligence is freely shared among the countries sometimes referred to as the Anglosphere. From there, I examine the period after World War II, in which interoperability and standardization are inculcated within NATO, considering how national militaries are turned into a coherent multinational force that is understood by many as the institutionalized military of the West. In the final case study I fast-forward to the recent past to examine the processes through which European Common Foreign and Security Policy (CFSP) is produced—not with an eye to how EU states shape that policy, but rather to how participation in that policy making reworks those states. Collectively, these case studies highlight how Britain has, over time, become enmeshed in multiple geopolitical assemblages that are productive of both pouvoir and puissance (the global diplomatic system, as well as assemblages that are perceived as the Anglosphere, the West, and Europe). Each of these processes provides an affective nudge to British policy makers, which collectively is perceptible at the macroscale. The cases I have chosen are insufficient to document every aspect of this complex, constantly-becoming-otherwise world of relations, but "all that we can do is attempt to capture snapshots of a constantly developing situation in the hope that it can reveal answers to the questions that we have, and illuminate the central features and interconnections in international relations."[69]

I selected these particular case studies (diplomacy, intelligence, defense, and the CFSP) not only because they represent the ways in which foreign policy has fragmented across various distinct parts of the state (or the supranational organization, in the case of the EU), but also because of the way in which these fields have been theorized in the literature. In each case, the literature has foregrounded the state as an actor, and a rational, autochthonous one at that. For instance, much international relations theory seeking to explain diplomatic action foregrounds the national interest as the rational basis for foreign policy.[70] The literature on intelligence cooperation similarly frames the exchange of intelligence through the language of quid pro quo, highlighting an economic rationality at the heart of the practice.[71] The literature on NATO interoperability is highly technical in orientation and focuses on the achievement of pouvoir without considering puissance (and of course uses neither term).[72] Finally, the literature on the CFSP generally sees it as the result of diplomatic negotiation without ever considering the way in which the policy repositions the collective subjects that compose it.[73] I do not spend much time reviewing these literatures not because the work is without insight, but rather because my starting assumptions are different, and also because I want to juxtapose these fields to generate conceptual and empirical insights, whereas these literatures tend to focus only inward at the phenomenon they take as their object.

The choice of Britain was both pragmatic (in that it is where I was based during this research) and a reflection of the historical nature of these assemblages. Britain has leveraged its period of historical hegemony into a lasting legacy of "centrality" within many geopolitical assemblages. However, every state's foreign-policy apparatus is embedded in these assemblages to some degree. It is the intensity of Britain's connections that marks it as a particularly suitable subject through which to examine the interconnection of multiple assemblages. The choice to produce a counterhistory of British foreign-policy making therefore reflects my belief in the importance of the past as a force in the present. While the past is hardly determinative of the future, it exists as a set of material resources in the present that shape the future's conditions of possibility.

In recent years, scholars have paid attention to the methods through which assemblages can be studied. Indeed, adopting assemblage ontology has implications for the ways in which we conceptualize research. Nick Fox and Pam Alldred argue that "the research-assemblage . . . comprises the bodies, things and abstractions that get caught up in social inquiry, including the events that are studied, the tools, models and precepts of research, and the researchers."[74] In short, and in parallel to earlier debates about ethical research and reflexivity, the researcher will affect that which is being studied (and vice versa). Further, the emergent outcome of research can ripple through wider social arenas, particularly if it is turned into policy. A reflexive approach to methodology offers the opportunity to reterritorialize the research-assemblage in ways that can lead to positive interventions in the world itself: "This micropolitical approach enables designs and methods to be engineered from the bottom up, and as interest in materialist approaches to social inquiry increases, offers a strategy for developing methodologies—both to understand the world, and to change it."[75]

The recognition that research methods can reshape the field of investigation has been recognized within critical international relations as well. Claudia Aradau and Jef Huysmans conceptualize methods as both *devices* and *acts*. Conceptualizing methods as devices foregrounds their role not as tools for observing truths, but instead in experimentation: "The device of extraction enacts worlds in the sense that it is an active force that is part of a process of continuous production and reproduction of relations, an endless process of bringing worlds into being."[76] Conceptualizing methods as acts highlights the ways in which the experimental spaces enacted through "methods as devices" can be stabilized into new orders, which disrupt and replace the old. "Understood in this sense, critical methods not only rupture knowledge, but also have the capacity to effect political rupture."[77] My research was designed to have this critical potential; to articulate the emergence of geopolitical assemblages is not simply an exercise in documentation or description. Rather, it is a *device* that makes this assemblage visible in a world that still largely attributes political agency in international affairs to the state, and not to the decentralized, rhizomatic networks of geopolitical assemblages beyond the state. This *act* holds open the possibility of reflection prior to political action, through which affects can be sensed and accounted for.[78] As William Connolly notes, we cannot escape the world of affect and achieve a disembodied rationality, but we can slow down and take note of the material contexts in which decisions are being made before rushing into mistakes.[79]

Methods

This research has been conducted via two methods: archival research and interviews. The challenge of accessing apparatuses of the national security state is real, particularly when dealing with contemporary issues. Access to currently serving foreign policy professionals in major states is notoriously difficult to negotiate, although the literature indicates that some exceptional results have been achieved.[80] For events in the distant past, it is easier to access archival sources and other accounts, such as memoirs. Interviews are often impossible as participants have passed on. For events in the recent past, interviews with retired national-security officials are appealing in that they often have in-depth knowledge and few competing time pressures. Some archival materials may be available, depending on the sensitivity of the issue. For contemporary events, it becomes necessary to rely entirely on interviews with serving or retired professionals, although some leaked documents may be available (as was the case with the intelligence-cooperation case study).

The cases I examine fall rather neatly into this schematic. I investigated the case study of the nineteenth-century British Foreign Office entirely through archival and secondary sources, namely Hansard (the U.K. Parliamentary record) and the U.K. National Archives. Approaching materiality through textuality has its own challenges, not least because of the way in which foreign-policy archives have been curated. For instance, the Foreign Office archives have been organized around foreign-policy issues, and little record of everyday life in the Foreign Office can be found in the National Archives.[81] "Just as we need to take into account and render transparent how the ethnographic researcher affects his or her reconstruction of associations, so do we have to grapple with the visibilities and invisibilities produced through the archive."[82] For this reason, parliamentary reports were particularly useful, as everyday life in the nineteenth-century Foreign Office is better represented in reports about budgets and facilities than in Foreign Office documents. I consulted early diplomatic memoirs to provide some hint of the lived experience.

My research on UKUSA intelligence cooperation was primarily archival, drawing from both declassified sources in the U.K. National Archives at Kew, the U.S. National Security Archive at George Washington University, and also leaked documents derived from the Edward Snowden affair. Despite the latter, my account contained substantial gaps, and so I supplemented the archival research with four interviews with retired intelligence officials in both the United States and United Kingdom as well as with one journalist who specialized in intelligence matters. These interviews provided insight into the embodied experience of participation in intelligence cooperation and the relationship between first- and second-order bodies politic. Per their request, the interviewees remain anonymous.

For the case study on NATO interoperability and standardization, I draw on archival research conducted at the U.K. National Archives and in the NATO Archives in Brussels. This allowed me to tack between national and institutional perspectives on the topic in ways that were highly productive; further, in the past specific documents were moved from the U.K. National Archives to the NATO Archives, indicating again how the specific history of archives can impact research design. My archival research was supplemented by two interviews with currently serving officials engaged in the negotiation of interoperability at NATO headquarters in Brussels.

The final case study, on the production of the CFSP in the wake of the Treaty of Lisbon, relies entirely on seven elite interviews. These interviews were conducted with retired and currently serving Foreign Office officials who engaged in the production of Europe policy, as well as European External Action Service and European Commission personnel who shape the production of the CFSP. I also interviewed "outsiders," including think-tank personnel linked to the CFSP and a research associate based in an EU delegation. For one of those interviews, I have respected the interviewee's wish to remain anonymous.

This methodology is not without weaknesses. For instance, for an assemblage analysis emphasizing embodiment, there is a dearth of real bodies in what follows. While some interviewees spoke directly to embodied aspects of their work, they did so, necessarily, at some remove. Similarly, the archival research offered up traces of embodied action more often than it did specific accounts of embodiment. For example, in the chapter on NATO interoperability, available documents detailed how idealized, normative bodies *ought* to perform geopolitically, rather than how specific, differentiated bodies *actually* perform geopolitically. Given the historical nature of much of this research, and the difficulty of interacting with bodies working within the security state, my methodology opens up the topic of embodiment, but imperfectly. One imperfection is the relative absence of women from this analysis; among all interviewees for this project, only one was a woman. While the national-security apparatus still skews male, it is obvious that the selection of interviewees is far from representative. This is even more true of the archival research, in which women barely feature at all. It is well known that women feature in national security in a range of ways that are not written into official records; given my dependence on the archive, this research has unfortunately reproduced that false absence.[83]

Hopefully this research design nevertheless inspires some readers to go further. Henceforth in this volume I eschew heavy theorizing in favor of a more empirically focused style. While each case study can be understood as a stand-alone venture, I read them alongside and against each other. I conclude by drawing together some of the similarities and disjunctures from these case studies and set out their implications both for the theoretical framework and for future studies in this area.

ONE

Materializing Diplomacy in the Nineteenth-Century Foreign Office

Much attention has been paid to how foreign policy matters, but significantly less has been paid to the *matter* of foreign policy. That is, foreign ministries, embassies, and various sites of diplomacy have been extensively considered via the symbolic dimension of architecture or location, but rarely in terms of their engineering or materiality (the exception being the literature on embassy security).[1] The logic of rational-choice theory and its variants within international relations generally discounts the bureaucratic-material context in which foreign policy is made, leaving no room for the bodies of ministers, diplomats, clerks, or others involved in the production of foreign policy, let alone the buildings they inhabit. In contrast, I foreground the foreign ministry itself as an assemblage of materials, bodies, and objects, subject to a range of processes unfolding at different temporalities. Understanding the foreign ministry in this way does not explain why specific foreign policies emerge from that assemblage, but it does help explain the force relations to which the foreign ministry—as an apparatus within the state assemblage and always also in assemblage with other foreign ministries—has been subject for the last two hundred years.

The British Foreign Office (known as the Foreign and Commonwealth Office since 1968) has long been a leader in the evolution of the modern diplomatic system. In fact, some theorists of the state have identified the creation of the Foreign Office in 1782 as a seminal moment in the formation of foreign policy itself.[2] Before the existence of the Foreign Office, there were two secretaries of state who conducted the king's affairs. They divided this labor according to a rough line that cut through England. The Northern Department was focused on the northern reaches of the kingdom as well as northern Europe. The Southern Department included southern England, Ireland, the Mediterranean, and the Americas. In short, there was no divide between domestic and foreign affairs. This changed, in 1782, with the creation of the Home Office and the Foreign Office, which bureaucratically rearranged the king's affairs to reflect the inside-outside distinction that has dominated understandings of politics ever since.[3] This is not to say that there was no distinction between domestic politics and diplomacy, because there was—albeit a less clear one than exists today. Rather, European diplomacy at the time was of a very limited intensity, with only a handful of ambassadors in London at the time. Further, diplomacy was essentially an aristocratic practice that required very little bureaucracy. There was not in fact much work for the Foreign Office to do, so foreign affairs was simply appended to the domestic responsibilities of the two secretaries of state.

British defeat in the War of American Independence marked a turning point for this genteel arrangement. Not only were the former colonies now states with whom the United Kingdom needed to establish diplomatic relations, but it was clear from the war that the bureaucracy of the British state was in need of reform. The world of foreign affairs was in need of more attention, and a dedicated apparatus was created in 1782 to attend to it. The new Foreign Office was founded next to St. James's Palace, on Cleveland Row, with just nine clerks and three servants to assist the first foreign secretary, Charles James Fox, in managing the affairs of state. Four years later, the Foreign Office alighted in Whitehall Palace, where it remained for seven years. Finally, it settled in Downing Street. The peripatetic relocations reflected the "new 'total' commitment of the country to the Revolutionary and Napoleonic Wars of 1793–1815, [which] enormously increased the number of staff required to run such large-scale military operations."[4] The bureaucratic challenge of running Britain's affairs was ramping up and would never again be the sleepy affair it once had been.

The Downing Street address situated the Foreign Office at the epicenter of the state's policy making. Comprising several adjoining private houses across from the homes of the prime minister and the chancellor, the Foreign Office benefited from proximity to power. It would seem to have been a perfect site in which to materialize the Foreign Office. However, the Downing Street Foreign Office would prove unable to materially accommodate the intensification of relations then occurring in the diplomatic system. Its lack of resilience to the force relations unleashed during this period of rapid change was a matter of concern for a whole generation of foreign secretaries, permanent undersecretaries, and members of parliament. As they debated where and how a new Foreign Office ought to be materialized, they sought to future-proof the new building against the intensifying affective forces of the diplomatic system by trying to imagine what capacities should be engineered into the facility. While the future of diplomacy was not, in fact, successfully extrapolated from the then contemporary trends, the capacities of the new building did in fact open up new potentials for the Foreign Office— and the practice of diplomacy more widely—into the present day.

I trace a traditional, anthropocentric account of the events surrounding the Foreign Office and its relocation to the current location on Whitehall. This account reproduces institutionalist histories by emphasizing human decision-making and agency. I follow this traditional account with a new narrative that deemphasizes anthropocentric agency and instead emphasizes the more-than-human nature of diplomatic practices and the affective forces that shape the spaces in which policy making occurs. In the first part of the new narrative I describe the ways in which paper was central to the everyday practices of foreign-policy formation and diplomacy in the nineteenth century, yet was also an unruly vector of affect. The circulation of paper through the diplomatic system affected the Downing Street Foreign Office in ways that ultimately unmade it. In the second part of the new narrative I consider the subsequent architectural debates over constructing a new Foreign Office on Whitehall, which centralized a specific concern for affective atmospheres and efficient governmentalities. In these debates, too, the circulation of materials (and the materiality of circulations) became a highly contested topic, pitting the greatest architects in the realm against one another in a controversy saturated with interdepartmental bureaucratic politics. I conclude by drawing out some implications of this historical case study for our understandings of time, power, and possibility. These implications will prove useful in the three more contemporary case studies that follow.

Historical Context

The historical account provided here is based on the reports of three parliamentary select committees that met to consider the state of the Downing Street Foreign Office and what to do about it; the events detailed in those reports (and in the secondary literature also examined) cover about thirty-five years, which will be detailed here to provide an overview. From 1793 the Foreign Office was located in five (later six) houses. These were 16–18 Downing Street (15 was added subsequently) and two houses behind them, fronting on the now disappeared Fludyer Street. By knocking through some of the internal walls and adding a new entrance by the architect Sir John Soane, the government adapted these houses for public service.[5] Over time, however, these offices proved insufficient, and the staff began to advocate for a new home. Lord Palmerston, a three-time foreign secretary and two-time prime minister, put the state of the Foreign Office on the government's agenda, and in 1836 the architect Decimus Burton was commissioned to design a new Foreign Office, to be also located in Downing Street. In 1839 the first select committee met to examine his plan, deeming it acceptable and endorsing it in principle. However, the rebuilding of the Houses of Parliament, which had burned in 1834, took precedence in the public finances, so the new Foreign Office building was shelved.

The complex on Downing Street continued to deteriorate during this interlude. After working for many years to maintain the building in working order, the first commissioner of works, William Molesworth, commissioned another architectural plan, having ultimately rejected Burton's plan for encroaching on St. James's Park. James Pennethorne, the official architect for the government, responded to the request, and in 1855 he presented a new plan to the second select committee. The committee agreed that the Foreign Office was in dire need of new facilities and endorsed the new plan. However, Pennethorne's proposal was shelved next to Burton's, as yet again public finances could not support a new building project. The Crimean War was eating up the funds that might go to a new Foreign Office. Ironically, this war exemplified the kind of foreign-affairs intensification that necessitated the new Foreign Office. Just as the American War of Independence and the Napoleonic Wars had led to greater organization and bureaucratization of foreign affairs—resulting in the initial establishment of the Foreign Office, in 1782—the Crimean

War sparked a further intervention into the material organization of the foreign-policy apparatus. It illustrated "the drawbacks of having a war directed from so many different buildings in London; rationalization became a popular cry, with a unified War Office becoming a major justification for a new government building."[6] For the second time, the context of foreign-policy making was rematerializing with an eye toward increased efficiency and therefore enhanced governmental reach beyond Britain's borders (*pouvoir*, a "concrete ensemble of relations").

At the time that Pennethorne's plan was shelved, Lord Palmerston moved across to 10 Downing Street. The former foreign secretary was determined to improve the state of affairs in his old department, and he commissioned three architectural competitions to that end. The first award would be for the best design for a new Foreign Office, and the second for the best design for a new War Office. The third award would be for a new, integrated design for Whitehall that would include both buildings. The competitions received 218 total entries, but it is hard to view the competitions as successful. The logical flaw of these competitions—that not all three could be built as at least one award conflicted with the others—served as the pretext for the third select committee, which met in 1858 to arbitrate between the three winning architects, who all expected their designs to be actually built. This was problematic as the winning plans for the Foreign Office clashed with those for the War Office (the two were to be located next to each other), and both by definition clashed with the comprehensive Whitehall design.

Eventually, the committee selected George Gilbert Scott, who had scored highly in all three competitions, to build a "palace of administration," which would combine the various foreign-policy apparatuses in a single compound. However, the War Office was ultimately built elsewhere, leaving the Foreign Office and India Office to share the two halves of the new facility. In June 1868, after a brief stint in Pembroke House (after the Downing Street building was demolished and before the new building was ready), the Foreign Office relocated into the Whitehall building. Scott was later asked to double the space of the new palace, and he added two new quadrants, which housed the Colonial Office and the Home Office (fig. 1.1).

But this was not the end of the story. During the twentieth century, the diplomatic system intensified on an exponential trajectory. World War I marked a massive uptick in the bureaucratic requirements of

Figure 1.1 George Gilbert Scott's completed palace of administration. Photo by Nigel Swales, used unaltered via a Creative Commons license (CC BY-SA 2.0).

foreign policy. The end of World War II sparked several rounds of decolonization that shifted the bureaucratic burden of governmentality from the India Office and the Colonial Office to the Foreign Office. The India Office was dissolved in 1947, and the Colonial Office was absorbed by the Commonwealth Relations Office in 1966. The Commonwealth Relations Office merged with the Foreign Office in 1968 to create today's Foreign and Commonwealth Office (FCO). As a result of these reorganizations, the FCO wound up sharing Scott's palace on Whitehall with the Home Office, which moved to Queen Anne's Gate ten years later. Today, the FCO occupies the whole facility and indeed spills out into other buildings, notably a facility in Hanslope Park, near Milton Keynes, as well as operating embassies around the world.[7]

The Diplomatic Archive in Everyday Life

The preceding account is a fairly traditional, institutionalist history of the Foreign Office and its facilities. While such an account is undoubtedly helpful, it follows in a long-standing practice of the social sciences: namely, imputing agency solely to the humans involved. Lord Palmerston, James Pennethorne, William Molesworth, George Gilbert Scott, and the various committee members are the idea men and the decision-makers, who engage in a rational allocation of resources to provide maximum benefit to their country. What follows now is an inversion of that account, in which these decision-makers are nudged and pushed in various directions by the affects circulating through the diplomatic system. To accomplish this, I emphasize the co-agency of materials alongside that of people, and also the ability of those material contexts to produce certain kinds of subjects. From this perspective, it is materials and their affective flows that animate human activity; at best the policy makers are trying to stay ahead of a rapidly changing material context. The fundamental material—although not the only one—is paper.[8]

Before I examine the specific relation of paper and the Foreign Office, I consider the more-than-human relationship between writing and political regimes in a longer historical arc, with a particular focus on diplomacy. Paul Adams traces the possibilities for governing at a distance that ancient writing, whether materialized on clay tablets or papyrus, enabled. The emergent result is a posthuman political regime, which he calls "kingship": "Kingship circulated as a quasi-object among network participants, functioning to maintain the stability of relations between, for example, stone masons, stones, toolmakers, slaves, soldiers, priests, nobility, crops, farmers, boat-builders, boat pilots and boats while the fixed or stabilized word functioned as an intermediary, linking rulers and all of these other things. Kingship expressed in disembodied form as a scribally linked network is a concept without scale."[9] The capability of writing to rework time and space varied with the materials on which words (or hieroglyphs) were written, as the coding of the writing enmeshed with the material capacities of the surface, and with those who read inscriptions, to produce new social effects. Kingship's parallel to transnational governmentality and the diplomatic-military dispositif are readily apparent. The importance of writing to diplomacy is embedded in the word itself: "Etymologically, . . . the word is derived from the ancient Greek word *diploun* (to double), and from the Greek word *diploma*, which refers to an official document written on double leaves (*diploo*) joined together and folded (*diplono*)."[10]

By the time the Foreign Office was founded, paper's advantages over other writing surfaces was evident with regard to diplomacy. Over the course of the 1800s, improvements in paper manufacturing flooded the market with inexpensive, wood-based paper.[11] All of this paper was able to circulate further and more quickly when it entered into assemblage with new printing-press and transportation technologies.[12] The advent of steam-powered transportation, in particular, enabled an intensification of kingship's reach to include the four corners of the globe. What made paper crucial to the practice of foreign policy was not just its ability to circulate widely, but more specifically its ability to circulate *and then accumulate* in an archive that could be accessed by policy makers. In early 1839, James Bandinel testified to the first select committee that access to the last twenty years' worth of paper was necessary to the everyday formulation and conduct of British foreign policy.

Rather than provide a technologically determinist account of the changes in the Foreign Office, however, I prefer to lay these developments in the world of paper and transportation alongside changes occurring in the diplomatic system contemporaneously. Indeed, the spread of paper through government was commonplace, occurring in other departments beyond the Foreign Office. It was changes in the diplomatic system that resonated with the rise of cheap paper to produce a problem for the Foreign Office. At the beginning of the nineteenth century, most of Central and South America gained independence from Spain, throwing open the relatively narrow world of diplomacy to a raft of new diplomatic subjects. As Joseph Planta testified to the first select committee, "When I first knew the office there were not above three or four foreign ministers accredited to this country; the number has now increased at least to four or five times that amount. Likewise, our relations with foreign countries were by no means as considerable as they are now; and latterly, in Mr Canning's time, the whole of South America was thrown open too, which almost doubled the business of the foreign office."[13] The sheer number of governments and ambassadors with whom the Foreign Office needed to interact meant that the office's work spaces had to accommodate an increased number of staff. Everyday work habits within the Foreign Office had to adapt to the presence of more people in the rooms, in the staircases, and so on. Beyond that, these bodies entered into relation with other elements of the Foreign Office assemblage—specifically, the paper.

Each of the three select committees pointed to paper as the crucial materiality within the Foreign Office assemblage. Indeed, it was impossible to preserve the Downing Street office precisely because it was completely incapable of dealing with the increased intensity of paper flows through the diplomatic system. The 1858 select committee heard evidence of this increased intensity of paper flows (see table 1.1). (It is notable that while the hearings took place after the invention of the telegraph, the Foreign Office had yet to install one of these devices— the next stage in the acceleration of communications of which steam-powered transport was the first.) Due to the massive influx of paper each year and the need to maintain access to these documents for twenty years, the paper-storage needs of the Foreign Office increased substantially each year, as the gap between the number of documents received twenty years before versus those received in the past year yawned wider.

The improvised solutions of the office's few decades had led to a material context that was hardly amenable to efficient policy making. Lewis Hertslet, the Foreign Office's longtime librarian and keeper of the papers, made this clear to the chair of the 1839 select committee.

> CHAIR: What is the extent of the library you have charge of?
>
> HERTSLET: The library consists of about 5,000 volumes, and the number of volumes of manuscripts now in the office is between 4, and 5,000.
>
> CHAIR: How are they placed?
>
> HERTSLET: They are placed in the most irregular and inconvenient manner possible; some of them are stowed away in obscure rooms and passages, and there is no semblance of a library.
>
> CHAIR: Are they all on the same floor?
>
> HERTSLET: No; they are on two floors, or rather on three floors, and these are distributed in the four or five houses of which the Foreign Office consists.[14]

Hertslet's son, who later served as the librarian as well and therefore saw the state of affairs in the latter part of this era, portrayed the library in his memoir as having shelves that are "three-deep," making it very frustrating to find the book for which one might be looking.[15]

This grim situation became grimmer in 1858, when Permanent Undersecretary Edmund Hammond in his testimony revised the archival needs of the Foreign Office, increasing it from twenty years up to thirty or fifty years.[16] The context in which this decision was made is highly relevant—it could simply have been a bureaucratic maneuver to gain more space for his department. Still, the fact that the need for paper storage seemed plausible leverage for Hammond indicates how central paper

TABLE 1.1 **The Increase in Dispatches Received by and Sent from the**
Foreign Office, 1821–1857

Year	Political Department		Consular Department	
	Received	Sent	Received	Sent
1821	4,379	1,630	—	—
1822	3,929	1,390	—	—
1823	4,893	1,909	—	—
1824	5,902	2,747	—	—
1825	5,635	2,740	—	—
1826	5,635	2,522	2,477	973
1827	4,135	2,002	2,456	966
1828	4,908	2,471	2,644	1,167
1829	4,565	2,033	2,274	874
1830	4,926	2,426	2,421	929
1831	5,889	2,510	2,949	1,513
1832	5,279	3,009	2,988	1,644
1833	5,529	2,815	2,536	1,689
1834	5,751	3,487	2,624	1,605
1835	5,487	2,928	2,954	1,664
1836	6,904	4,268	3,226	2,055
1837	6,881	4,503	3,449	1,942
1838	7,511	5,163	3,213	1,584
1839	7,892	5,535	3,234	1,796
1840	8,426	6,032	3,324	2,001
1841	8,922	5,574	4,484	1,813
1842	8,192	4,533	5,461	1,882
1843	8,363	4,597	5,309	1,784
1844	8,615	5,032	5,279	2,136
1845	7,989	4,280	5,353	2,310
1846	8,951	5,442	5,112	2,257
1847	10,755	7,483	5,215	2,415
1848	10,565	7,772	5,323	3,030
1849	11,705	7,660	5,800	3,081
1850	11,358	8,892	5,638	3,071
1851	11,511	8,705	6,186	3,914
1852	11,902	7,835	6,292	3,734
1853	13,143	9,120	6,565	3,826
1854	17,969	15,661	7,436	5,562
1855	18,855	17,246	9,543	9,571
1856	19,719	17,340	10,427	7,606
1857	20,268	19,057	9,979	7,313

Slave Trade Department		Total		Grand Total, Received and Sent
Received	Sent	Received	Sent	
155	29	4,534	1,659	6,193
175	116	4,104	1,506	5,610
101	80	4,994	1,989	6,983
391	246	6,293	2,993	9,286
390	294	6,025	3,034	9,059
474	321	8,586	3,816	12,402
427	275	7,018	3,243	10,261
382	259	7,934	3,897	11,831
451	563	7,290	3,470	10,760
494	350	7,841	3,705	11,546
409	307	9,247	4,330	13,577
299	197	8,566	4,850	13,416
313	260	8,378	4,764	13,142
427	395	8,802	5,487	14,289
595	474	9,036	5,066	14,102
693	472	10,823	6,795	17,618
745	403	11,075	6,848	17,923
848	687	11,572	7,434	19,006
1,128	1,056	12,254	8,387	20,641
1,257	946	13,007	8,979	21,986
1,740	1,514	15,146	8,901	24,047
1,911	1,781	15,564	8,196	23,760
1,854	1,910	15,526	8,291	23,817
1,926	1,558	15,820	8,726	24,546
2,169	2,029	15,511	8,619	24,130
1,604	1,619	15,667	9,318	24,985
1,461	1,537	17,431	11,435	28,866
1,327	1,323	17,215	12,125	29,340
1,379	1,100	18,884	11,841	30,725
1,506	1,175	18,502	13,138	31,640
1,678	1,320	19,375	13,939	33,314
1,252	1,028	19,446	12,597	32,043
1,344	1,115	21,052	14,061	35,113
1,269	953	26,674	22,176	48,850
1,166	938	29,564	27,755	57,319
1,556	1,266	31,702	26,212	57,914
1,599	1,307	31,846	27,677	59,523

was to the debate. Indeed, the select committees all expressed concern at both the sheer amount of paper being stored and the lack of fireproofing in the Downing Street office.

In this scenario, paper was a flammable hazard so abundant it hindered its own usage; that is, there was so much paper in the Downing Street Foreign Office that it was difficult to access the right papers. These properties of the Foreign Office archive led to inefficient public service. However, there were bigger problems that can only be understood by looking at the way in which the paper interacted with the lived experience of foreign-policy making on Downing Street. As Andrew Barry writes, "The political significance of materials is not a given; rather, it is a relational, a practical and a contingent achievement."[17] It was the specific assemblage of materials that composed the Foreign Office that led to the emergence of the problem. One of these materialities was the alluvial soil on which the Downing Street office was built. Henry Seward, the surveyor of works and buildings, testified to the first select committee: "I know there was formerly a ditch running along very near the centre of that mass of buildings, taking the old front of Sir Samuel Fludyer's house, and, running between the houses in Downing Street and Fludyer Street; it was an ancient sewer, therefore the ground on each side of it is bad."[18] Given that the Foreign Office was composed of houses that fronted Downing and Fludyer Streets and backed up against each other, this testimony suggests that a pre-Victorian sewer ran directly beneath the middle of the building.

Another relevant materiality was the Foreign Office building itself. Originally built as a series of houses for private use, the Downing Street office was not built to specifications for a public office. While individual sheets of paper are useful for being lightweight, stacked and bound paper is relatively heavy even in small volumes. As Lewis Hertslet testified, the Foreign Office was literally stuffed with paper, which placed a great load on the structure. Because the clerks often ran in and out of the office, they maintained workspaces close to the ground floor, while paper was initially stored on the higher stories. The architect Thomas Chawner testified in 1839 that this arrangement contributed to the instability of the building, and so the papers were moved to lower floors.[19] This displaced the clerks and contributed to the collective frustration regarding inefficiency as the clerks had to climb more stairs to do their jobs.

The risk posed by the paper's weight was magnified by the adaptations originally made to the houses when they were converted into the

Foreign Office. Interior walls had been removed to facilitate movement and communication within the office, and this weakened the structure in ways that left it ill-suited for bearing such a load. Henry Seward spoke to the 1839 committee about the complex's least stable house, formerly owned by Sir Samuel Fludyer: "There has been an alarm about this house in consequence of the alterations made with a view to meeting particular calls for accommodation, laying the rooms together, and taking away walls; and it likewise appears that the bow front to the west is considerably crushed in the lower part, in consequence of the heavy weights which have been thrown upon it."[20] The improvised solution to the Foreign Office's earlier spatial-relations problems had helped to create the problem now facing the Foreign Office. Further improvisation—in the form of posts fitted in the middle of rooms to support the floor above—helped, but replicated the original problems.

The final material element in this assemblage was the printing presses. For the same reasons that the paper had originally been stored aloft, the printing presses had originally been located on the upper story. These printing presses were constantly in motion—back and forth, side to side—because the Foreign Office not only had its own printing to do, but was also the confidential printer for other government departments. The long-term effect of the mechanical motion of these large, vibrating machines—in the attic of these sagging, overloaded houses built on weak soil—was the drastically uneven settlement of the Foreign Office. This was entirely predictable, as Chawner testified in 1839: "I found a great quantity of types used in printing; these they moved from one place to another, which I consider improper; if great weights are shifted from one place to another, it is likely to cause settlements."[21]

As a result of the 1839 testimony, the presses were moved into the basement and the paper was relocated as much as possible onto the lower floors. However, the memories of past immoderations were materialized in the building. As several of the party walls descended further into the earth, it became impossible to open doors; one end of a room could be a full foot lower than its other end. The doors were constantly being rehung in an effort to make them workable. It was a Sisyphean effort for the government's engineers to keep the building in public service. When the other houses on Downing Street were taken down during this period, it became clear that the Foreign Office building had been dependent on those houses to remain upright (fig. 1.2).

Fludyer
Street

Foreign
Office

Colonial
Office

Downing
Street

Privy Council Office

ASPECT OF THE OLD FOREIGN OFFICE FROM WHITEHALL

Figure 1.2 The Downing Street Foreign Office, dependent on struts after the neighboring houses were taken down. From Edward Hertslet, *Recollections of the Old Foreign Office* (London: John Murray, 1901).

The heightened intensity of diplomatic communications—in the form of paper—thus affected the material infrastructure of the Foreign Office, resonating with the extant properties of the building. The poor foundation and the improvised architecture would not have necessarily been a problem for the operation of the Foreign Office had these flaws not been activated by the constant motion of the printing presses in the attic and the accumulating weight of paper. While these processes necessarily unfolded over decades, they manifested in events that signaled the structural changes and inspired fears not only for inefficiencies in the public work but also for the safety of those working in the Foreign Office. Two-time foreign secretary Lord Malmesbury "was made perfectly aware of the physical state of his new department in the most tangible way when part of the ceiling of his room fell onto his desk."[22] The diplomatic archive was not only a primary cause of this trouble, but also at risk as a result. A wall enclosing a fireplace once collapsed, allowing fire to splash into the reference room, which was (like most rooms) heavily laden with paper. Even a small fire in that room would have crippled the materialized institutional memory of the Foreign Office for generations (and a "small fire" in that context would be unlikely).

In this account I have emphasized the co-agency of paper in literally shaking the Foreign Office to its foundations; from this point of view, the diplomatic archive is not just a tool to enable foreign policy and the production of a transnational governmentality (pouvoir), but also a material force that shapes human action (puissance). In this case, the problem that paper posed to the British foreign-policy apparatus required investing in a new building that would be safer and more efficient than the last. In the next section I turn to the debates over what kinds of material affordances would provide a resilient home for the Foreign Office in a rapidly changing diplomatic assemblage.

Architecture and the Affective Atmospheres of Efficiency

One step removed from the safety concerns of the Downing Street Foreign Office was concern about its *inefficiency*. From the beginning, when interior walls were removed to facilitate movement and communication within the office, everyday life in the Foreign Office involved overcoming the frustrating architecture that resulted from combining five (and later six) houses into a functioning public office. Debates over the design of the new office that featured in the 1858 select-committee testimony can thus be understood as being about producing particular affective atmospheres. Architectural design can contribute to the production of affective atmospheres, as it "enables the channeling of affects through configurations of fields that architects and buildings intend to, and sometimes do, create."[23] These configurations of fields require the governance of circulations, as Foucault noted in his lecture on apparatuses: "It was a matter of organizing circulation, eliminating its dangerous elements, making a division between good and bad circulation, and maximizing the good circulation by diminishing the bad."[24] The new Foreign Office was to be a space defined by its strict territorialization; the circulation of bodies coded as "Foreign Office" ought to be enabled as much as possible within the new building, while bodies coded as "other" ought to be excluded as much as possible from the work spaces in order to facilitate an affective atmosphere of efficiency. However, this alone would be insufficient for an atmosphere of efficiency: the walls of the Foreign Office ought to—as much as possible—enable light and air to permeate the space within.

With regard to the strict territorialization of the Foreign Office, a parallel to the coding of bodies can be found in the issue of paper. One proposed solution for the Foreign Office's paper problem was to store all paper in the State Paper Office, which was built nearby in 1833. This solution was roundly rejected on account of the Foreign Office's unique working practices.

> CHAIR: Have you occasion to refer often to the papers of a distant date?
> HERTSLET: I cannot say that we have; but we should more often refer to them if they were easier of access [i.e., not in the State Paper Office]; for it not infrequently happens that references are required at a late hour of the day—for instance, Parliamentary references—that must be reported upon forthwith; there is then no time to send to the State Paper Office; and if there were, the State Paper Office was probably shut, even before the question arose; and we are compelled to do the best we can with imperfect materials.[25]

Here is a claim that the temporality of daily life in the Foreign Office does not resonate with that of other government departments. The work of the Foreign Office tends to be later in the day, while the State Paper Office closes at 4 p.m.

The strict delineation of the Foreign Office from other government departments stretched to the governance of bodily circulation as well. Just as the Foreign Office papers could not mingle with those of other departments, it was desirable that those working in the Office should likewise not mingle with others. Permanent Under-Secretary Hammond made just this case when discussing the layout of a future building with the committee:

> CHAIR: You would have your office self-contained?
> HAMMOND: Certainly. Our office is quite large enough for any one set of servants to manage; and especially as regards office hours; our sys-

tem in the office is so thoroughly different from that of every other office, as far as I am acquainted with other offices, that we never could combine our arrangements with those of another office.

CHAIR: Then you would not like even a door into the Colonial or any other office?

HAMMOND: No. I should, in the first place, particularly dislike the facility of communication between the clerks of different offices, from the circumstance, among other reasons, that our real business hours, that is hours of pressure, commence when other offices are rising, and it is a very natural thing for acquaintances from one office to come into the other office just at what would be to us the most inconvenient time. In fact, I would much rather have as few visitors in the office, and as little encouragement to visitors, as there could possibly be.[26]

This strict territorialization—of bodies and papers—is predicated on an understanding of the discordant interactions that are possible between offices that operate at different temporalities. To force their integration would be to undermine the efforts being made to produce an affective atmosphere of efficiency.

In contrast to this rigid inside-outside distinction for bodies and paper, Hammond argued for a building interior that both minimized the need for movement and facilitated it where necessary. Hammond's plan is obviously haunted by the Downing Street office, in which movement was frequent and difficult. As an example of the inefficiency this produced, Hertslet the younger notes in his memoirs that the librarian's office was located on the first floor, while the reference room was downstairs and on the other side of the building. Hammond testified similarly about life in the old Downing Street office: "The divisions are scattered all over the office; three of my political divisions out of four are in the second storey; and if I want to speak to one of the clerks, I must either bring him down to me, or if I want to refer to a paper or the register in the department, I must go up myself."[27] Imagining a new, utopian building with an affective atmosphere of efficiency, Hammond envisioned an idealized hierarchical space of communication: "All our clerks should be together; that is to say, every division should be complete in itself. The senior clerk should have one room for himself and one or two other clerks, and the juniors should be in a room going out of it, and those rooms should be as much as possible in direct communication with the Under-Secretary of State immediately superintending the division to which that senior clerk belongs."[28] Sketched out in this way, Hammond has materialized the professional hierarchy of the Foreign Office in the horizontal dimension to facilitate movement. When asked by the committee about the number of floors he would like the new building to have, he asks for three but cannot express what would be found on the other two floors. His eventual answer—that the slave-trade department and passport office could be located in the basement and the translator and the treaty department could be located in the attic—materialized yet another hierarchy, this time in the vertical dimension. These departments were less integrated into the daily workings of foreign-policy formation.

The 1858 select committee, as it debated the various architectural proposals before it, confronted a controversy over which of the winning designs was most permeable to light and air. Hammond argued before the select committee that "the great object in a public office, as far as the interior is concerned, is to have as much external air and as much external light as possible."[29] This was entirely congruent with contemporary thinking vis-à-vis the city and its moral geographies, and indeed the select committee accepted Hammond's proposition as commonsensical.[30] Spatial design was understood as enabling the development of certain moral subjectivities—such as that of the efficient worker. Hammond's focus on the *public* office tacitly implies that private houses have less need for such engineering. Hammond's more demanding standard for public buildings was again haunted by the Downing Street experience; the lack of circulation (of all kinds) within the old office was the byproduct of its original design as a series of private residences. As with the governance of bodies, inasmuch as greater circulation of light and air could be materially designed into the new building, the Foreign Office could achieve an atmosphere of efficiency.

Hammond's request to the select committee was for voluminous windows that would allow light and air into the building, as well as for no courtyard in the center of the building. He made the latter request both because he believed that the sound of carriages turning in the courtyard would echo throughout the building, undermining the atmosphere of efficiency, and also because the air in the courtyard would stagnate and prevent fresh air from entering the building. Hammond's claims regarding the courtyard were thoroughly debunked by all three architects (the final plans included a courtyard). The remaining discussion centered on which kind of window would enable the greatest amount of light and air to enter the building, a topic on which there was considerable disagreement.

Henry Coe (who received the first-place prize for the Foreign Office design) and Charles Barry (second prize) both used Italianate design, while George Gilbert Scott (third prize) deployed Gothic design. Coe and Barry both argued before the select committee that Gothic design, with its intricate employment of mullions to fragment the windows into many smaller panes, limited the amount of light and air that would enter the proposed building. Indeed, Barry—the son of Sir Charles Barry, who designed the new Gothic-style Houses of Parliament—noted that this was not just his and Coe's opinion, but also "the frequently expressed opinion of gentlemen with whom I have necessarily come into contact in this very building in which we sit, when I was acting for my father."[31] In short, the committee members themselves should consider how well-liked their own building was and use that to inform their opinion of the Foreign Office designs before them. This was an effective argument because during the summer the stench of the Thames (just outside the Houses of Parliament) required all windows to be shut, turning Parliament into an oven.

Whereas Barry relied on this form of instinctive, anecdotal form of argument to carry his case, Scott relied on scientific evidence. His argument was that Gothic windows could be wide enough to compensate for the mullions, and that new technologies—such as window sashes—enabled Gothic windows to match Italianate in terms of the circulation allowed. To puncture the stereotype of Gothic windows as narrow he introduced a slate of statistics comparing window sizes in a range of well-known Gothic and Italianate buildings in London. After dispelling the prejudiced commonsense around Gothic windows, he then introduced his own commonsense argument: "As to the windows, the capability of window light in the Gothic considerably exceeds the capability in Italian architecture. I may mention that if it had not been so, it would have involved a great absurdity in the conduct of our forefathers here, and their contemporary architects in Italy."[32] In other words, it makes no sense at all for a gray and rainy country (England) to be home to an architectural style that limits the amount of light that enters, while a sunny country like Italy would be home to light-maximizing architecture. In his closing argument, Scott argued that a major government building ought to be built in the indigenous style rather than one introduced from abroad.

This coding of the Gothic style as "national" offered a mode of argumentation that did not hinge on the various styles' potential for affective atmospheres. This proved important; the select committee in the end decided that the two styles in question did not materially impact the amount of light and air that could enter. Architectural style therefore no longer impinged on the state's interest in an atmosphere of efficiency. Further, given that the new building was to be located between the Gothic Houses of Parliament and the Italianate Horse Guards Parade, the architectural coherence of Whitehall was not in question. The lack of criteria left the subsequent decision to the personal whim of Lord John Manners, the head of the Board of Works. Being a fan of the Gothic style, he selected George Gilbert Scott's design. However, the election of Lord Palmerston as prime minister undermined Manners's decision: as an ardent anti-Gothicist, Palmerston required Scott to redesign the building in the Italianate style. (It is understood that Scott made the Italianate windows smaller than he could have as a form of subtle protest.)[33]

Time, Power, and Possibility

The slow-motion collapse of the Downing Street Foreign Office and the debates over the material form of the new building on Whitehall bear all the marks of a tedious story: it is after all a tale of the public sector that unfolds over the span of decades. Nevertheless, it provides a window into the power of the nonhuman in a world of diplomacy that too often assumes a humanistic ontology. The challenge of studying the more-than-human is one of space and time; in order to perceive the agency of materials we must be willing to look to spaces and times that are both infinitesimal and vast in comparison to those normally examined in our anthropocentric conceptualization of diplomacy. For example, the destruction of the Downing Street office was the result of a range of material processes unfolding at different temporalities and yet resonating with one another. A pre-Victorian sewer undermined buildings that were originally built as private homes decades prior to their conversion into public offices. At the same time, the initial wave of decolonization in Latin America led to an intensification of the diplomatic system just as revolutions in paper manufacturing and steam transportation came online. These processes were linked through the everyday life of the Foreign Office, which brought together these processes in a single mundane site. The escalating flow of paper, combined with the vibration of printing presses and the steady footfall of clerks running up and down the stairs, led to the slow-motion collapse of the building and inefficiency in the diplomatic work conducted therein. This inspired the government to open up the public coffers for a new facility that would materialize the Foreign Office in a specific form that would be expected to last well into the future. The effect of this was to provide opportunity for the leadership to reterritorialize the Foreign Office in a material context productive of atmospheres of efficiency that insulated the apparatus from external puissance while maximizing the state's pouvoir in the world. The debates that unfolded in the select committees emphasized the material contexts of the old office and the imagined new one; at issue were the impacts of courtyards, window sashes, and printing presses on the efficiency of the Foreign Office. The fact that the 1858 select committee ultimately came to a nondecision is less important than the fact that the technologies of architectural design were collectively deemed vital to the state's interest in the affective atmospheres of the Foreign Office.

In the introduction I conceptualized traditional diplomacy as a form of transnational governmentality that shapes the subjectivities of both those who work for the state and those beyond the state. Scholars of governmentality tend to conceptualize the archive as a technology of power, but this has usually been done in a way that abstracts the archive from the actual materials that compose it. As a result, the archive becomes simply a tool of the governmental apparatus and not an actual thing, with the capacity to affect and therefore also with agency. However, the archive is not only crucial in *effecting* governmentalities but also in *affecting* them. In the Downing Street Foreign Office, not only the archive itself but also the means of its reproduction shaped the affective atmosphere in which policy making occurred. This experience haunted the development of the Whitehall Foreign Office, and produced a space that opened up new lines of flight not only for the Foreign Office but for the wider field of diplomatic practice. The desire to future-proof the Foreign Office by constructing a building resilient to changes in diplomacy inspired extra space to be set aside for the storage of paper; eventually all four parts of Scott's "palace of administration"—with all their storage capacity— would fall into FCO hands as well. Still, as indicated by the recent public acknowledgment of a million colonial-era files that had been illegally

kept from public view in a "lost" archive in Hanslope Park, paper continued to flood the Foreign Office well beyond its material ability to sustain
and organize its own archive.[34] The "lost" files occupy fifteen miles of
bookshelves that stretch from floor to ceiling; such volume could not
have been provided for in any of the "future-proof" architectural plans
considered by the 1858 select committee. The shift to a digital office in
recent decades is not, however, a dematerialization of the archive. It is a
rematerialization in the form of computer memory, servers, and broad-
band networks. The materiality of this archive affects the FCO and its
embodied subjects just as paper did; the specific nature of that relation
is an empirical question that has yet to be asked or answered.

In this chapter I have opened the door to an examination of foreign-
policy making in which diplomacy is not simply the way in which
policies are enacted or advocated after they have been devised; rather,
diplomacy is an openness to the outside, or an affective relationship
that is always already inside the policy-making process. Therefore, foreign
policy apparatuses are constantly becoming *with* their various interlocutors. Diplomats themselves can be the conduits for this affect, a point congruent with Costas Constantinou's claim that diplomats are the tendons
of the diplomatic system.[35] However, it is important also to move past the
humanism of Constantinou's argument to consider a more-than-human
diplomacy, in which the agency of paper, telegraph cables, diplomatic
gifts, and other infrastructure of diplomacy are brought to center stage.
This is not merely a gesture of inclusion, but a radical rethinking of the
diplomatic subject: from a rational actor seeking the national interest to an
affected and affecting body whose subjectivity is emergent from a range of
processes unfolding over a range of temporalities.

Diplomats themselves might object to this treatment; it might feel
disabling or like an evacuation of political agency and responsibility. If
agency is everywhere and in everything, and diplomats are themselves
the product of their environments, how can diplomacy achieve anything?
I counter that an understanding of how geopolitical assemblages unfold
and interact with one another is crucial to knowing the microgeographies
and microtemporalities in which diplomacy can be deployed successfully to achieve a desired outcome. Connolly describes those who have
attuned to these affective currents as seers: "A seer does not only express
premonitions about an uncertain future at protean moments. Those
same skills and sensitivities are also indispensible to the formation of

new maxims, judgments, concepts, and strategies at untimely moments when a collection of old precepts, habits, and standards of judgment are insufficient to an emerging situation."[36] In short, an understanding of diplomats as seers stresses the role that diplomats play at the outer edge of the state apparatus. Like finely tuned antennae, diplomats will feel the flux and flow of "foreign" affects most immediately, and therefore might be the first to sense when the rules of the game are changing and new opportunities are present. Highlighting this skill accentuates, rather than abdicates, the responsibility of diplomats to produce "new maxims, judgments, concepts, and strategies at untimely moments."

Indeed, time and the untimely have been a constant through this chapter. The untimely burning of the Houses of Parliament and the Crimean War prevented the British government from dealing with the slow-motion crisis in the Downing Street Foreign Office when it was obviously a hindrance to good foreign-policy making. Similarly, it was the decades-old material heritage of improvised choices with regard to the Foreign Office that resonated with moments of innovation in paper manufacturing and steam transportation to affect both the physical structure of the building and the atmosphere within it. Attempts to locate power and agency within such a complex assemblage are a challenge to scholars. The decisions made during the period under consideration here might seem to be merely ham-fisted attempts to influence events beyond policy makers' control. However, the movement of paper to the National Archives and the so-called "digital transformation" of the FCO has freed up space within the new building to do things other than store paper. This material capacity has enabled a growth in staff numbers and therefore an increasing specialization. Whereas staff in the nineteenth-century Foreign Office largely served as clerks, working with all this paper—"Almost all the junior clerks did similar work and spent their days copying, ciphering and deciphering, 'blueing,' and indexing"—today's FCO includes a wide array of specialists, including social-media managers, economists, and lawyers.[37] The capacity to accommodate a staff of roughly 4,500 has opened up new bureaucratic capacities for action that would have been inconceivable in the nineteenth century. This, in turn, ripples through the wider world of diplomacy as foreign ministries adapt to each other's innovations. The FCO has emerged as a pioneer of the new specialist, network-oriented diplomacy that marks the twenty-first century.[38] The traditional anthropocentric association of agency with intent inspires us to link power and agency to human timescales in which change might be effected. We can say whether an attempt to exercise power was successful by evaluating whether a positive outcome was achieved within a reasonable amount of time. However, the open-ended relational spaces of assemblage call on us to consider time as open-ended as well. The temporalities of more-than-human processes are not necessarily "reasonable" or even easily perceptible by humans bound to an embodied sense of time. The happy outcome of the current FCO as a world leader in diplomatic innovation is, in part, a result of the decisions made with regard to its material context dating back to the period examined here.

The remaining chapters of this book will draw on the insights garnered in this chapter: that the microgeographies and microtemporalities of everyday life and the macrogeographies and macrotemporalities of the diplomatic system are constantly becoming together, sometimes resonating in ways productive of lasting emergent effects and sometimes passing by each other. I now turn to one such moment of transformation: the advent of intelligence cooperation between the United States and United Kingdom during World War II.

TWO

UKUSA Signals Intelligence Cooperation

In November 1942 Alan Turing, the now-famous British cryptographer and one candidate for inventor of the modern computer, was on a train from Washington to New York City. Having been let into the United States to see the American industrial effort at decryption, Turing was now on his way to Bell Laboratories to examine a new ultrasecret American device that could encrypt telephone calls. However, the American officers in charge of the project had been ordered to maintain confidentiality, and Turing was refused entry. It may have been acceptable to collaborate on decryption with allies, but encryption was central to the national security state's ability to maintain its *own* secrets. When British officers approached Colonel Crawford, the Army Signals Corps officer in charge of the telephone-scrambler project, he clearly informed them that Turing would not be allowed to see it. Turing's subsequent departure for New York therefore only proved an irritant for the improvised wartime relationship between the intelligence apparatuses of the erstwhile allies.

Such is the nature of intelligence cooperation during wartime; even allies are suspicious of each other, as information is power and today's ally might be tomorrow's rival. For this reason, a substantial percentage of existing literature on intelligence cooperation draws on rational-choice theory to imagine an economy of intelligence.[1] In this particular case, however, specific problems beyond the rational made it difficult for the intelligence apparatuses to mesh.

Turing's famously prickly personality aside, the affect of suspicion that attached to Turing as he toured the U.S. intelligence effort seemingly resulted from the manner in which he went about his mission. Turing himself described the situation in his report to London.

> There was some trouble because no arrangements for me to see anything other than unscrambling projects had been confirmed in writing, whereas I had come out on the understanding that I was to see everything there was in the way of speech secrecy work. Dr. Murray was very friendly about it and said that if it were confirmed from the right quarters in England that this was what I intended to do, then he could fix it. . . . As soon as we had gone Murray started to get on with arranging things for me but immediately came up against a veto on any British people visiting anything at all in the speech scrambling line.[2]

Turing's expectations of informality stemmed from his background in the British signals intelligence (SIGINT) effort, which was centralized within the Government Code and Cipher School (GC&CS, now known as the Government Communications Headquarters [GCHQ]). The American SIGINT effort, however, was fragmented between the State Department, the army, and the navy, and was therefore more difficult to navigate. The American view of the situation is perhaps best summed up by an internal memo from Major General Strong of G-2 (U.S. Army SIGINT): "Instances of this kind will constantly occur until the British are educated to the degree of putting all the cards on the table and to dealing with responsible officers instead of going on their own and snooping with underlings. If the British cannot be frank and, on secret information, deal on the proper level after having been properly introduced and accredited, they can expect no other treatment than they have received."[3] The emphasis on formality, hierarchy, and accreditation in Strong's account was an institutional response to the fragmentation of decision-making and power within American signals intelligence at the time. It is not surprising that Turing would be lumped in with a larger critique of the British as freelancing and nomadic.

This anecdote is not historically significant, but it is telling with regard to the barriers that had to be overcome in order to create today's UKUSA assemblage. As recent disclosures by Edward Snowden have detailed, the signals intelligence agencies of the United States, the United Kingdom, Canada, Australia, and New Zealand together form a transnational assemblage composed of circulating data, affects, and other materials. Within this assemblage there is near-total sharing of both raw intelligence and encryption-decryption technologies. This assemblage does not take the form of an institution (unlike NATO or the EU) but is instead reproduced through bureaucratic routines in each country's SIGINT apparatus and materialized in a range of materials such as drones, satellites, and microwave transmitters. It is notable that what brought Turing to the United States in 1942 was a concern with encryption devices such as the telephone scrambler and decryption devices such as the bombe devices being produced in the United States. Signals intelligence, despite its ethereal-sounding subject matter, is a profoundly material enterprise with regard to the technologies of mediation, the technologies of eavesdropping, and the embodied subjects whose practices animate the intelligence apparatus.

In this chapter, I trace the ways in which UKUSA came together in the context of World War II and survived into the Cold War era. This process of assemblage is unique in the world of intelligence cooperation and is worthy of examination. I then shift my attention to the embodied routines that enabled affects of trust to eventually replace the suspicion that stuck to Turing when he liaised with his American counterparts in 1942. In this discussion I focus largely on the production of protocols that enable *puissance* (constitutive power) among first-order bodies politic (UKUSA workers), looking at the engineering of bureaucratic microgeographies. I then examine *pouvoir* (actualized power) and consider the technologies of mediation and eavesdropping over time, as well as how those changing materialities have shaped the capabilities of UKUSA. The geography of communications infrastructure proves to be of paramount importance here. I then return to puissance, but from the perspective of the second-order bodies politic of the UKUSA states and their intelligence apparatuses: how were these institutions and their foreign policies affected by participation in UKUSA? I conclude by summarizing my empirical findings and their relation to my larger argument about civilizations and flat ontology. I also argue for continued theoretical engagement with the field of intelligence studies.

Origins of UKUSA

Identifying an origin point for any assemblage is not a challenge; instead, the challenge lies in choosing from the many possibilities. The coming together of things, people, and ideas necessary to produce something as unlikely as UKUSA requires attention to a whole range of processes unfolding over different temporalities. A conventional history of UKUSA might start with the official diplomacy of states; one such origin point would be a message from the British government to that of the United States dated 5 September 1940, in which it was suggested that the two states resume their intelligence cooperation from World War I.[4] This would take the form of a complete exchange of information on German, Italian, and Japanese cryptography, as well as an ongoing swap of radio intercepts.[5] The United States agreed to the exchange of information but not of intercepts (which would wait until January 1943). This split decision was likely influenced by the fact that the United States was not yet at war; still, it began the process of aligning the intelligence apparatuses of the two countries toward each other in anticipation of future alliance. This origin point therefore has some appeal, not least because it carries within itself the seeds of its own destruction as an origin by pointing back to U.K.-U.S. intelligence collaboration in World War I.

An assemblage approach to UKUSA, however, requires us to look beyond the top-down politics of state institutions. Indeed, another origin for UKUSA can be found in the theater of war, where collaboration between U.S. and British troops was improvised and where the benefits were more immediately tangible than at the abstract level of policy makers. For instance, the Office of Strategic Services (predecessor to the Central Intelligence Agency [CIA]) compared notes with British intelligence in Southeast Asia throughout the war.[6] Such informal information exchange was so satisfactory that the U.S. Navy initially resisted any formal agreement: "While in effect we actually collaborate on all technical matters, we are not bound by any agreement to do so. For example, although we have agreed to supply all recoveries we have not promised to supply our methods in making recoveries."[7] Both formal and informal forms of intelligence cooperation had occurred before, in World War I, and had ceased with the end of hostilities. What was different now?

Two factors loomed large in the decision to maintain wartime collaboration into peacetime. First, peace looked elusive as the armies of Europe closed in on Berlin. As the western front swept through Germany, the boffins of Bletchley Park (where GC&CS was housed) and Arlington Hall (where U.S. Army signals intelligence was housed) were armed and jointly sent on what were known as TICOM (target intelligence) raids. These mathematicians and decryption experts swooped in to seize German cryptographers and decryption equipment so that they could continue working against the Soviets, but with new masters.[8] The same thing happened in the Pacific theater, although there the raids happened separately and the results were shared afterward.[9]

The postwar "push" to eavesdrop on the Soviets was not just because the United States and the United Kingdom perceived them as a new rival, but also because the advent of atomic warfare meant that the future could no longer be seen as an extension of the past. A radical rupture in time had occurred, and for policy makers the past no longer offered lessons that could be used in the present. In short, the atomic bomb—in affect-imbued images of mushroom clouds, strategic-planning reports, and first-person accounts of Hiroshima and Nagasaki—entered into state foreign-policy assemblages in ways that were anxiety producing for policy makers. SIGINT, however, offered hope of seeing into the future and preempting crises.[10] This joint desire by policy makers on either side of the Atlantic to shape the future required the redirection of the wartime collaboration toward the Soviets. The new intelligence project was first known under the code name of RATTAN and later as BOURBON.

The second factor which helps to explain why RATTAN was a transatlantic project was the material infrastructure of communication in the late 1940s. The primary mode of governmental communication at the time was radio, which shaped the geographies of eavesdropping in certain key ways.[11] With the British Empire having regained most of its former extent (at least for the moment) in the Mediterranean and South Asia, and the United States having seized new territories in the Pacific, the two states together could achieve near global coverage, with listening stations all around the world.[12] However, this somewhat simplistic reading of the topography of empire and radio must be laid alongside an understanding of the topologies of the telegraph network, of which London was the heart: "British intercept stations are more favourably located than ours to copy certain RATTAN traffic. In addition, RATTAN traffic passed on British-owned cables would be available."[13] To a certain extent, this collaboration was about global interception of radio signals and full access to secure telegraph cables, but it also reflected the difficulty of cracking Soviet codes. World War II cryptography was a volume business, in which the sheer number of intercepts could be used to help crack the code by making patterns more obvious. Therefore, by sharing intercepts, the United Kingdom and the United States made it statistically more likely that one of them would be able to achieve a breakthrough (which would also be shared).

Nevertheless, these factors did not guarantee the collaboration would continue. There were calls at the time to exactly avoid the mangling together of U.S. and U.K. foreign policy that I have made my subject in this volume: "We will find ourselves disadvantageously placed if we have to support GREAT BRITAIN always vis-à-vis RUSSIA. I feel the technical advantages gained by this collaboration are entirely insufficient to warrant any possible hamstringing of our proper position in the international structure."[14] Such sentiments, however, were distinctly a minority view in a government that was already looking toward postwar rivalry with the Soviet Union.

Uncertainty about the future worked both against the collaboration and for it. One such uncertainty was over resources that would be available during peacetime. The U.S. and U.K. SIGINT apparatuses had been relatively well provided for during the war, once it became clear how crucial their activities were. After the war, it was obvious to everyone that budget cuts were on the horizon, but what was less clear was which country's SIGINT apparatus would be more affected. One American officer argued bullishly that "in the latter part of the war we have had to share considerably more than our share of the load.... Unless a proper bargain is struck with the British, it is probable that this state of affairs will persist and we shall find ourselves at the short end of things."[15] Contrarily, a senior American naval officer argued, "I feel that not long after the peace, [the British] will outstrip us in communications intelligence—not in what we *might* do, but rather in what we *shall be allowed* to do."[16] Such uncertainty made the quid pro quo of rational-choice theory a difficult prospect; the institutionalization of the wartime SIGINT collaboration was therefore an event saturated with affect: trust earned on the battlefield, anxiety about the future, and gut instinct.

Diplomatic meetings between intelligence officials from both sides of the Atlantic commenced in October 1945, and a framework agreement was signed on 5 March 1946. But this was only the beginning of the diplomatic wrangling, as the working procedures of this unprecedented collaboration had yet to be worked out. Those procedures were established in a series of technical conferences that created and amended the appendixes to the UKUSA agreement, which were in many ways the substance of the partnership. These appendixes give insight into the everyday diplomacy that occurs within the UKUSA alliance.

The Time-Spaces of Intelligence Work

The agreement set in train a process in which the U.S. and U.K. SIGINT communities mangled together. More specifically, it meant the integration of specific institutions—originally GC&CS, the U.S. Army Security Agency, U.S. Naval Signals Intelligence (Op-20-G), and so on—via a variety of technologies that linked them and enabled new circulations to occur. At the scale of everyday work, this entailed a harmonization of security procedures, jargon, and material forms. For instance, the formatting of raw intercepts and analytic reports, the brand of equipment, the methods of encryption, and so on served as protocols linking the agencies involved in UKUSA. While these protocols allowed for intelligence and other forms of knowledge to circulate within the resulting body politic, it also opened up the potential for bodies working within the assemblage to be affected. In this assemblage, bodies were territorialized and coded in particular ways.

The first appendix added to the UKUSA agreement harmonized the code words to be used to describe specific categories of intelligence, as well as the associated procedures for keeping them secure. CREAM referred to decrypted intelligence circulating within the UKUSA assemblage, while IVORY referred to traffic intelligence (information that could be gleaned without decrypting a message) circulating within UKUSA.[17] The UKUSA agreement was a secret *even within the participating organizations*, with these two categories being the highest level of classification; to know about CREAM or IVORY was to know about UKUSA itself. The production of an information hierarchy resulted in a stratification of the material form of the intelligence itself. Because CREAM was top secret, it could be transported unencrypted only when "sealed and via officer courier or other trusted routes, . . . or by protected in-house local communications systems, or by external landlines only as specifically approved."[18] IVORY was, by contrast, classified merely as secret. Therefore, in addition to the above routes, registered mail was an acceptable form of transport. Neither CREAM nor IVORY could be "conveyed by aircraft or land transport over territory controlled by other than the United States or British governments."[19]

But the secrets of the state are not just written down; they are embodied in key individuals within the assemblage. Both the United States and the United Kingdom were expected to limit the number of people who were indoctrinated (sworn in) to UKUSA. CREAM and IVORY could only be handled by the indoctrinated, and therefore the microgeographies of the workplace were rearranged: "Due precautions shall be taken (by providing segregated, secure areas or otherwise) to ensure that the activities and knowledge of such persons are confined to the COMINT [synonym for SIGINT] material and activities to which they have access."[20] If space was designed in such a way as to preserve the UKUSA secret, so was time: "Every effort shall be made to ensure that no person who has a knowledge of current value about COMINT, such that his capture or interrogation could be a substantial risk to the security of COMINT, shall be assigned to or engage in activities of a hazardous nature."[21] The temporality of the word *current* is clearly linked to the nature of the knowledge possessed. Staff was coded by security procedures as occupying four different categories. Those in the first category were entirely unaware of UKUSA, and therefore their mobility was limited to spaces where CREAM and IVORY were not present. Those in the second category knew about IVORY, while those in the third knew about IVORY *and* CREAM. Staff in the second category could not be assigned to hazardous duties (where they might be captured by the enemy) for six months after they last handled intelligence, and staff in the third category could not be thus assigned for a year. Those in the fourth category were so integral to UKUSA activities—"precise knowledge of COMINT processing techniques, competence, or potential"—that they could never be given hazardous duty again.[22] Therefore, both the material forms of intelligence and the bodies of those who handled it were coded in ways that were productive of a series of striated spaces from the scale of the office to the scale of the world map, and also of striated times from the microtemporalities of the everyday office to the lifetime ban on hazardous duty.

Of course, the ultimate purpose of UKUSA was not to separate things and bodies, but to bring them together in a new transnational context. The security measures produced striated space-times with the intention of unleashing new flows through the smooth space of UKUSA. This was clear in the agreement, which defined "foreign communications" as those of "a faction, group or nation that is not a party to this agreement."[23] The blurring of boundaries between the United States and the

British Empire was a purposeful exercise in reworking the political sub-jectivities of those working within it. As an intelligence "insider" has noted, one of the reasons for UKUSA's success is that those who *use* the shared intelligence do not know from which country it came.[24]

The blurring of the foreign and the domestic enabled by UKUSA re-quires an intensity of mutual trust that is not normally associated with intelligence agencies. Arguably, it may have been possible to institution-alize UKUSA after World War II only because of the degree of trust that had been earned on the battlefields of Europe and the Pacific. While these affective relations could be perceived at a range of scales, from the soldier to the heads of state, trust often stuck to particular bodies, which were key in the moment of institutionalization. For instance, one U.S. Army officer relied on his wartime experience of British Foreign Secre-tary Bevin in his assessment of the British proposal for UKUSA: "He has debated vigorously and sometimes harshly before entering into [agree-ments], but having once committed himself he would carry out his con-tracts to the full."[25] However, the war was in the rearview mirror, and UKUSA could not rely on the trust built up during the war; UKUSA had to organize its spaces in a way that was productive of an alternative form of transnational intimacy.[26]

One such method, adapted from the war collaboration and incorpo-rated into the UKUSA agreement, was secondment: "Each party is au-thorized, with the consent of the other, to send personnel to work with the personnel of the other party on any task allocated to such other party or for which it may be responsible."[27] This practice continues to this day and is responsible for the production of community within UKUSA. One retired British senior official described it as "a massive ex-change of people coming back and forth all the time for talks. . . . The key players will all know each other, from the mid-career on up."[28] A dif-ferent but similarly senior U.K. emeritus official noted that the manage-ment boards of the U.S. National Security Agency (NSA) and of GCHQ hold a conference together once or twice a year, and specialist groups frequently get together to discuss their fields—"cryptographers hold-ing conferences about elliptic curves or other mysterious things which I never understood."[29]

The physical proximity brought about by secondment and other simi-lar practices made it difficult to keep secrets. While the UKUSA agreement allowed secrets if they were deemed to be in the national interest, it was clear that too many such secrets would undermine the project. There-fore, proximity meant that while secrets could be kept, the existence of those secrets—if not their contents—would likely be known. This raised the stakes for keeping secrets to the point where only national-interest concerns of a high order would be deemed worthy of risking the trust that had accrued over time among the SIGINT professionals.

And, indeed, the physical proximity of secondment and frequent conferencing led to bonds of trust and friendship that formed over the course of a career. These bonds served as an affective reservoir that could be drawn on if necessary, as a retired U.S. intelligence official ob-served: "Friendship requires having a reserve; 'you know you can trust me because I haven't done this to you before this.' With the Common-wealth it just makes it easy, it's comfortable and you know you can trust one another even though you recognize you work for another coun-try."[30] Therefore, the microgeographies designed into the UKUSA agree-ment helped to maintain and diffuse trust, which had at first been overly centralized in bodies like those of Bevin.

The ambassadors of UKUSA are the senior liaisons, whose job de-scription is laid out in Appendix G of the original document. These individuals are based in each other's headquarters and serve as con-duits for official requests for information or aid. Further, there is a pro-liferation of liaisons who are accredited to specific working groups or agencies as needed. Therefore, like secondment, liaisons serve to put SIGINT professionals in close proximity for long periods of time, and indeed they "shall normally have unrestricted access to those parts of the other's operating agencies which are engaged directly in the production of Communication Intelligence."[31] This level of integration allows rela-tionships the time to produce an affective reservoir—one retired U.K. senior intelligence official described it as "growing up together," with friendships often originating in some common posting in an obscure location and continuing as the friends climb the career ladders of their respective bureaucracies. "In the SIGINT world you have life-long friend-ships that extend into families, into holidays, because people don't know anybody else. You are in this business for life."[32] Having established the role of affect and embodied professionals in producing the UKUSA as-semblage over time, I now turn to the role of communications technolo-gies in enabling a range of relations that compose UKUSA.

Technologies of Media and Eavesdropping

A more-than-human approach to UKUSA directs our attention to the role of nonhuman elements in the political agencies that emerge from processes of assemblage. The relevance of the nonhuman to UKUSA is particularly evident in the communications media that are both central to the transnational links that make UKUSA possible and also the object of UKUSA surveillance. Indeed, the UKUSA assemblage incorporates not only the cables and databases that link allies, but also the cables and databases that link "foreign" governmental apparatuses.

With regard to the "internal" media that allow intelligence cooperation to cohere, there is a long history of attentiveness on the part of UKUSA elites. In January 1944 these elites discussed the creation of the Britain–United States of America (BRUSA) circuit, which would link together U.K. and U.S. radio systems to allow messages to flow freely from one side of the world to the other: Washington, Pearl Harbor, Melbourne, Colombo, and London. Of course, this topology of connection had to coexist with a topology of disconnection, through which secrecy could be maintained. "Crypto-channel 34" of the circuit was set aside for the exchange of Japanese signals intelligence.[33]

The development of common methods of encryption and decryption to be used in crypto-channel 34 and elsewhere was predicated on the proliferation of material objects that could mediate between the existing systems. The American ECM Mark II and the British Typex cryptographic devices were both based on a rotary mechanism that spun whenever a character was keyed into it, encrypting the message via an algorithm materialized in the rotary. To link these encryption-decryption networks required the distribution of new rotaries throughout the network. The resulting Combined Cipher Machine (CCM) crystalized the wartime cooperation in material form, serving as a protocol that opened up the two SIGINT assemblages to each other's affective forces (fig. 2.1).

The creation of the BRUSA circuit was only the beginning of the evolution of the UKUSA communications network. Even as the war ended, both the United States and the United Kingdom agreed that the existing communications infrastructure was insufficient for the scale of collaboration envisioned.[34] In its 1946 iteration, Appendix H specified that new circuits would supplement the old and that the old circuits be channelized to increase their capacity. These changes enabled a greater *intensity*

Figure 2.1 A Typex 23 device, modified for use with the Combined Cipher Machine (note the "MODIFIED" stamp on the rotary box behind the keyboard). Photo by Tom Murphy, used unaltered via a Creative Commons license (CC BY-SA 3.0).

of information flows between the capitals. In its 1953 iteration, Appendix H included new text: "Lateral communications between stations of one party and Agencies or stations of the other" may be provided.[35] This is evidence of the increasing *density* of the information flows, with information circulating through a rhizomatic network with less regard for the hierarchy of capitals; collaboration was becoming more decentralized and unfolding in a range of topological spaces.

The densification of the UKUSA internal network was paralleled by the increasing number of connections between UKUSA and its constituent outside. While it is possible to lay both forms of quantitative intensification alongside one another, it is important to remember the *qualitative* difference between the internal and external relations of UKUSA: the internal relations were meant to produce an unimpeded flow of information between government apparatuses, while the external relations were hierarchical in that they were intended to eavesdrop while maintaining UKUSA secrets. Necessarily, changes in media technology altered the geography of eavesdropping. For example, the rise of satellite communications called for a different UKUSA infrastructure than the network of listening stations that had helped to jumpstart the collaboration in

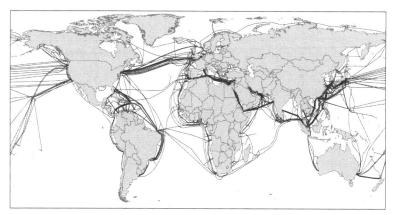

Figure 2.2 A map of the undersea fiber-optic cables composing the modern-day communications infrastructure. Map by Miles Irving of the University College London Drawing Office, using source data made available by Greg Mahlknecht at http://www.cablemap.info.

World War II. The first three satellite listening stations were located in friendly locations where commercial communications networks downloaded data from satellites after traversing the oceans: Cornwall, West Virginia, and Washington state. However, today the density of world communications requires more satellites and more listening stations. As recently as fifteen years ago, the NSA was operating ten or eleven listening stations within the "footprints" of communications satellites.[36]

However, not all technological change is so macroscaled; even as satellite technology shifted attention to a few satellite footprints in which mass surveillance could be conducted, the rise of microwave radio communications (the basis of mobile-phone technology) necessitated a new microscaled network of listening stations within urban areas. Fortunately, this network could be grafted onto existing material infrastructure: the embassies and consulates of UKUSA and other friendly states.[37]

The most recent front in UKUSA efforts to keep up with changes in communication is fiber-optic cable, the geography of which generally replicates the topology of the old telegraph network (thus reiterating the centrality of the United States and United Kingdom) (fig. 2.2). The difference lies in the materiality of the cables themselves. Unlike radio, microwave, or satellite signals, which can be "tapped into" without indication, fiber-optic cables channel signals composed of light, which deteriorate if a tap is put on the cable. Because the signal deteriorates, eavesdropping can be detected. However, recent revelations indicate that an NSA program called STORMBREW takes advantage of U.S. centrality to the fiber-optic network, tapping the cable (seemingly without degrading the signal) at seven sites where the physical cable enters U.S. territory. It is unclear exactly what technology makes this "upstream" collection possible. However, "downstream" collection has been widely reported as well, such as the NSA PRISM program, through which data is collected after the fact from Internet companies such as Google or Facebook, either overtly or covertly. It has even been reported that the NSA intercepts the deliveries of computer servers that have been purchased by Internet companies. Once intercepted, these servers are opened up, tampered with, resealed and delivered with no notice of the "back door" that has been inserted in the computer architecture.[38]

Of course, getting data has always been the easy part; as in World War II, the challenge is to defeat the encryption that has been used to mask the message. Several programs exist to try and stay ahead of the commercial and publicly available forms of encryption that exist. For instance, "PROJECT BULLRUN [is] a joint effort between the NSA and [GCHQ] . . . to defeat the most common forms of encryption used to safeguard online transactions."[39] Similarly, "EGOTISTICAL GIRAFFE . . . targets the Tor browser that is meant to enable anonymity in online browsing."[40] Another alternative is to collect data *prior* to the moment of encryption, for instance via malware. One such program is called Quantum Insertion; it catalogues keystrokes in order to see what a user is typing, then sends the keystroke log to the NSA. Through techniques such as this, as well as downstream methods of data collection, non-UKUSA computers are embedded in a network of material relations. This is no trivial point: the servers of such prominent e-mail service providers as Google and Yahoo! have been infected with Quantum Insertion, as have over fifty thousand private computers. The technological components of the UKUSA assemblage range from the tiniest malware programs to the enormous field of geometric radomes at the Royal Air Force base at Menwith Hill (fig. 2.3).

If the geography of SIGINT has often reverted to historical precedents—for example, the mirroring of the telegraph and fiber-optic networks—one change in the SIGINT world has no precedent: the intensification of communications flows in recent decades. "As of mid-2012, the [NSA] was processing more than twenty billion communications events (both Internet and telephone) from around the world *each day*."[41] This inten-

Figure 2.3 The radomes of the UKUSA satellite listening station at RAF Menwith Hill, 2005. Photo is in the public domain.

sification poses problems for both analysis and archiving. With regard to analysis, the sheer number of intercepts renders human processes of sorting and interpretation impossible. New technologies, however, work to enable analysis. For example, XKEYSCORE is a software package that enables the analysis of e-mail and metadata that are skimmed via the processes such as STORMBREW and PRISM and stored on roughly 750 servers in 150 cities. XKEYSCORE appears to be the newest version of a software package that had long been rumored to exist: ECHELON.[42] Another software package, BOUNDLESS INFORMANT, visualizes the incoming data streams in real time in order to render them immediately actionable.

With regard to the archiving of all this data—and of other flows necessary for analysis—it is clear that the SIGINT agencies struggle with capacity in a way that parallels the nineteenth-century Foreign Office's struggles with paper. The rapid intensification of communications means that, for reasons of space, the bulk of communications must be deleted prior to being analyzed. In late 2013 the NSA opened a $1.5 billion data center in Utah in hopes of storing data a bit longer in case it is needed, but given the historical precedent of the Foreign and Commonwealth

Office building in Whitehall, one wonders how long this center will last before it, too, requires supplementation.[43] Another problematic flow is that of electricity; in January 2000 a power-supply breakdown led to the collapse of the NSA's analytic capabilities, with all data being rerouted to GCHQ for analysis for three days. Other, smaller breakdowns go unreported for reasons of national security, and so it is unclear how resilient the UKUSA assemblage is.

As the changing intensity of communication flows has challenged the ability of the SIGINT agencies to keep up, the agencies have gone from being communications-technology innovators to chasing the digital avant-garde, which is in the private sector. Of course, speaking of the private sector (companies) in contrast to the public sector (UKUSA) is itself the kind of binary that assemblage theory tends to disregard. Beyond the overt and covert incorporation of corporate Internet servers and private computers into UKUSA, private contractors have become enrolled in the assemblage as providers of new technology and even of Open Source Intelligence (OSINT): "Initially focused on business intelligence, companies have moved into mainstream security to meet the capacity problems that emerged after 9/11."[44] This market is controlled by a very few privileged corporations who usually have just one customer: the U.S. government.[45] Further, the growth imperative of capitalism, once mingled with the (trans)national security state, affects the perception of the "national interest." As Glenn Greenwald notes, "Companies like Booz Allen Hamilton and AT&T employ hordes of former top government officials, while hordes of current top defense officials are former (and likely future) employees of the same corporations. Constantly growing the surveillance state is a way to ensure that the government funds keep flowing, that the revolving door stays greased."[46] Conceptualizing UKUSA as the mangling together of second-order bodies politic is a useful maneuver because it also allows us to account for the movement of first-order bodies politic between the UKUSA governments and their privatized security apparatuses.

Further, this maneuver allows us to deemphasize the purported leaders of the UKUSA assemblage—the SIGINT directors or their political masters—in favor of a decentered approach that flags up corporate and other interests that affect the UKUSA assemblage (puissance). We might instead think of these elites as engaged in constant, desperate efforts to order the elements of the assemblage and direct its agencies toward desired targets (pouvoir). This narration of the assemblage flies in the face of the popular imagination, which views spy agencies as omniscient protectors of the public. (Hence the quiescence in the face of domestic spying; many are oddly reassured that their spy agencies are capable of such invasive surveillance of their lives.) However, the unruly elements of the assemblage are constantly threatening to undermine this capability: the megaflows of intelligence which threaten cascading systems failure, the financial demands and brain drain of private contractors, and the new modes of encryption that constantly emerge and threaten UKUSA's ability to monitor communications.

While the historical development of UKUSA has helped it accrue a fair degree of political coherence, it operates in an unstable context. For instance, many SIGINT officials in the United States who are not directly involved in the collaboration (and therefore miss out on secondment and the other affective techniques of trust formation) either think that the United States should have no privileged partners or assert others (such as Germany) as better choices. Further, the NSA-GCHQ partnership is tighter than other institutional relationships, such as that in the world of HUMINT, or human intelligence (the CIA and MI6). This makes broader U.K.-U.S. intelligence sharing difficult, as the HUMINT and SIGINT agencies often have different orientations to UKUSA partners. A senior CIA official described a difficult situation posed by UKUSA during the Falklands War: "GCHQ seems to share everything they get from the NSA with [MI6], and we [the CIA] would give the NSA something that is NOFORN [not for foreign distribution] and they would say we can't do that—our system is not set up that way."[47] Indeed, UKUSA protocols have filtered into the coding of the software packages involved. This is unique even within the U.K.-U.S. "special relationship," as a retired MI6 official told me: "The NSA-GCHQ infrastructure is *sui generis*. Logically on the broader intelligence front there wouldn't be interlinked computer systems."[48] Therefore, the UKUSA assemblage requires careful maintenance with regard to all its relations, both human and nonhuman.

I addressed the engineering of affect among individuals and the microspaces of intelligence cooperation before moving on to the technological elements of the assemblage relating to communications, both internal UKUSA communications and those through which the alliance eavesdrops on its constituent outside. In the next section I turn to the impact of these microscaled practices of assemblage on foreign-policy

formation, both in terms of how it affected the foreign-policy apparatuses after World War II and in terms of the policies that have emerged
from those apparatuses in the intervening decades.

Affecting the State

As SIGINT cooperation bubbled up during World War II and was formalized in the UKUSA agreement after the war, a complex process of
mangling-together or puissance enabled the intelligence agencies to affect one another, subtly reworking not only their institutional structures
but also the larger state assemblages of which they were but a part. Even
during the war, British and American SIGINT institutions were coordinating personnel decisions. For example, when Op-20-G (U.S. naval
signals intelligence) had a shortage of Japanese translators a month before VJ Day, they asked the British to "not reduce the scale of their effort
until the Japanese emergency [was] over, as they provide[d] a reserve
of skilled and experienced personnel."[49] The SIGINT agencies were thus
beginning to territorialize each other's elements even before the war
ended. The formalization of the UKUSA agreement accelerated this process, with this reterritorialization generating change within each of the
five allies' state assemblages. The relationality of this affective relation is
evident when one juxtaposes the changes wrought in the U.S. SIGINT
community with the changes occurring simultaneously in the SIGINT
community of the British Empire.

For the U.S. SIGINT community, joining UKUSA generated affects that
pushed the community into a more centralized apparatus. During the
war, there was no single SIGINT bureaucracy in the United States, with
the army and navy each possessing their own SIGINT capabilities and infrastructure. "Though the two cryptanalytic organizations shared code-
breaking responsibilities, cooperation was the exception rather than the
rule."[50] The State Department also conducted its own SIGINT operations. By contrast, the British SIGINT effort was centralized in GC&CS
(now GCHQ). The fractured nature of the U.S. SIGINT establishment
led to a disjointed front in negotiations with the British during the war.
For instance, Arlington Hall (army SIGINT) had a stronger operational
relationship with British SIGINT than did Op-20-G (navy SIGINT). So
when Op-20-G declined to share intelligence with the British, the British would simply ask Arlington Hall to get it from the navy. This lead to
feuding between the U.S. Army and Navy, and even a brief suspension

of intelligence sharing between the two branches of the military *during wartime.*[51] Obviously, this situation was not sustainable.

As interactions with the British intensified, and as formalizing cooperation rose on the agenda, it became clear that a single negotiating partner had to be found to represent U.S. SIGINT. Therefore, the State-Army-Navy Communications Intelligence Board was created, with representatives from each of the three branches of government involved in SIGINT; this board was a direct parallel to the London Signals Intelligence Board (LSIB), with whom negotiations would be conducted. This move had important implications for the U.S. armed forces, as by 1953 all U.S. SIGINT activities had been centralized in the new National Security Agency—a counterpart of GCHQ. Only over a long period of time would the U.S. armed forces regain their own SIGINT capabilities, which today remain secondary to the NSA in importance. Thus, UKUSA led over several years to the centralization of U.S. SIGINT along the lines of the British institutional model. However, this does not mean that the British SIGINT community remained unaffected; UKUSA ultimately led to the decentralization of the British Empire's SIGINT even as it replicated the British institutional SIGINT model.

The geographical advantages that collaboration with the British Empire had for the United States was based on British claims that they spoke for the SIGINT communities in the United Kingdom, Canada, Australia, and New Zealand. A draft of the eventual agreement, in 1945, includes this claim, despite the fact that no dominion SIGINT agency agreed to be subordinate to the LSIB.[52]

The reason for this lies in the dominions' complicated and unusual path to independence, which took on the trappings of sovereignty gradually, over the course of a century.[53] The relationship of the dominions to the U.K. at this particular point in time produced a topological conundrum. The dominions were simultaneously in the UKUSA agreement as parts of the British Empire, yet beyond it as independent countries. The United States generally favored the simplicity of a single contact in London for all SIGINT collaboration, as the wartime experience of collaborating with the dominions had been rocky.[54] Similarly, the LSIB "felt it should have a preferred position as regards the dominions and desires to exercise the right of approval regarding United States contacts with dominion agencies."[55] However, the U.S. Navy—still dragging its heels over the agreement—insisted on explicit approval by the dominions, which was eventually obtained in a side room of a Commonwealth Intelligence conference. The fuzziness of this compromise is embedded in the eventual text: "While the Dominions are not parties to this Agreement they will not be regarded as third parties."[56] This compromise wording proved temporary, and by 1953, all three dominions were fully independent actors within the UKUSA alliance.

Still, before this could happen, the dominions' SIGINT capabilities had to be reworked in order for the dominions to mesh with the new UKUSA model as full partners. The dominions' stand-alone SIGINT capabilities were minimal. For example, British SIGINT personnel were responsible for leading the Australia–New Zealand Integrated Communication Intelligence Center in Melbourne. Further, the three dominions' SIGINT agencies had little in the way of counterintelligence capabilities, which rendered them weak links in the maintenance of the UKUSA secret. Australia specifically was prohibited from full participation after Russian KGB and GRU infiltration was discovered.[57] A new counterintelligence agency, mirroring the British MI5, was established in Canberra to clean house and enable eventual full Australian membership in UKUSA.[58]

In other ways the dominions altered their SIGINT apparatuses to mesh with the emerging UKUSA model. A Canadian intelligence document explicitly positions their postwar reform as rooted in the combination of U.S. and U.K. models: "In general the tendency is towards greater control by the Foreign Office and the State Department . . . in planning the structure we might draw from the experience of both countries though our governmental system is somewhat different than both and so we cannot transplant the whole from either."[59] In the end, Canada created a single SIGINT organization—as the United Kingdom had and the United States would soon have—called the Communications Branch of the National Research Council. Australia created a Joint Intelligence Committee along the same lines as the British committee of the same name, as well as "a unitary Signals Intelligence Centre along the lines of GCHQ, which was given the cover name Defence Signals Branch [DSB]."[60] The mirroring of the British was so complete that staff were seconded from GCHQ to launch the organization, including the DSB's first director.[61] UKUSA thus not only centralized American SIGINT capabilities (to the detriment of the armed forces), but also helped the dominions gain the trappings of the national security state, thus speeding their departure from the defense umbrella of the British Empire. Nevertheless, those trappings were distinctly British in form.

The impact of UKUSA is not limited to the bureaucratic structures of the intelligence agencies; it also impacts the larger processes of foreign-policy formation in which those agencies are embedded. Maintaining the intelligence capabilities of UKUSA has in fact become a foreign-policy objective in its own right: "At remote locations such as the Chagos Islands in the Indian Ocean or Ascension Island in the Atlantic, the future of entire territories was shaped by the need for Anglo-American listening stations. Intelligence had once merely served the 'special relationship' but now secretive intelligence and defence projects lay at its very centre."[62] In other words, the maintenance of particular territories as listening posts is itself a foreign-policy objective, one which carries a cost for the United Kingdom. At least three of Britain's fourteen remaining Overseas Territories—the Chagos Islands and Ascension Island, plus the Sovereign Base Areas in Cyprus—are maintained largely for purposes of SIGINT collection. The complete depopulation of the Chagos Islands at U.S. request (for security reasons) continues to be a black mark on the United Kingdom's human-rights record.

Beyond this, the circulation of affects within UKUSA can be understood as a driver of common perspectives on foreign policy. As the former intelligence official Sir Stephen Lander argues, "The UK Weekly Survey of Intelligence and the Presidential Intelligence Brief probably look very similar most weeks and that tends to reinforce the closeness of the world view of the two governments."[63] John Dumbrell articulates this phenomenon as an "inclining logic" that nudges policy makers in all five countries toward similar positions and makes it difficult to chart different paths, noting that it was "practically impossible to disentangle U.S.-U.K. sharing of military intelligence regarding Argentina" in 1982.[64] But it is important to not overstate the power of intelligence cooperation; Dumbrell also notes in a counter-example that the British failure to intervene in the Vietnam War illustrates how this convergence of views is highly contingent on circumstances. Similarly, Richard Aldrich notes that while Western intelligence agencies agreed that Iraq had weapons of mass destruction in 2003, they by no means universally lined up in favor of invasion.[65]

It is not the common intelligence that produces common foreign policy, but rather the processes through which common intelligence is produced. It is these processes that shape not only the intelligence but also the subsequent interpretation of the intelligence by embodied policy makers. Other forms of everyday diplomacy can resonate with the processes of intelligence cooperation to create an intense field of affect that produces empirical effects on policy making. For instance, in an interview a senior U.K. intelligence official argued that the close links between the U.S. and U.K. executive branches contributed to the 2003 invasion of Iraq.

> [Blair] having committed himself morally, . . . the railway timetables of war meant that most of the British Army was in the process of being deployed to the Gulf before any [Parliamentary] decision was actually taken that the UK was going to participate, because they couldn't afford to wait. . . . Having had our military planners integrated with U.S. military planners, we were an integral part of the U.S. military plan. . . . So are we going to say, "Sorry, we are not coming?" This would have been unthinkable.[66]

Rather than any single field, it was the overlapping and resonating diplomacies of defense, intelligence, and so on that together produced an emergent policy on either side of the Atlantic. Other outcomes were of course possible, as was demonstrated in the 2013 Parliamentary vote on Syria.

The 1946 meetings at which UKUSA took form were in some ways about building an infrastructure that would enable British and American statesmen (as they all were at the time) to grasp and control the new, atomic future. They could not have imagined the media technologies and computational infrastructure their organizations would be dealing with today.[67] However, they did foresee the ways in which it would mangle the two countries together. Major General Sir Stewart Menzies, head of MI-6, noted in 1946 that UKUSA was significant "both in ensuring cooperation in the SIGINT field and in its effect on cementing the relations between the two countries generally."[68] Indeed, nearly seventy years later another senior British intelligence official told me that UKUSA was "right at the center of the U.S.-UK relationship. It is the connection between the two and the reason for the special relationship."[69]

Drawing on secondary literature, original archival research, and interviews with retired intelligence officials and freelance journalists who cover the intelligence world, I have documented in this chapter the genealogy of the UKUSA assemblage and its subsequent evolution over the past seven decades. The singularity of the UKUSA phenomenon in the world of intelligence is worthy of reiteration; nowhere else in the world are intelligence agencies as enmeshed as they are in this case, and with good reason. In this genealogy I have highlighted the specific spaces and times in which this cooperation originated—the battlefields of World War II, the rise of atomic weapons—as uniquely suited to the emergence of UKUSA. This was a highly contingent set of events, difficult (but not impossible) to imagine being replicated today. The recent failed attempt by the United States and Germany to forge a similarly close intelligence relationship demonstrates this. To cooperate in encryption and decryption is to render it (nearly) impossible to maintain secrets of your own.

The assemblage approach makes it clear that rationalist approaches to intelligence cooperation (in which quid pro quo exchange is emphasized) fail to grasp the phenomenon in all its complexity. A government's decision-making power must be laid alongside other human and more-than-human agencies involved in intelligence cooperation: private companies, changing media technologies, and lone-wolf actors like Edward Snowden, to name a few. The role of affect in shaping the subjectivities of political elites such as intelligence officials and foreign-policy makers has been too often occluded, as have the baroque technicalities that enable affects to circulate. These include all the procedural, technical, and analytic protocols that were adopted in the appendices to the UKUSA agreement and which evolved over time: the original rotary of the Combined Cipher Machine, the XKEYSCORE servers, the secondment programs, the formatting of analytic reports, the common Russian-English dictionaries, and so on. It is these everyday interactions between SIGINT agencies that intensify the links various first-order bodies politic, first- and second-order bodies politic, and various second-order bodies politic in a way that both reproduces the state as an actor in international affairs and generates something bigger than the state: a geopolitical assemblage that lacks any bureaucratic center but is instead an emergent agency acting back on the elements composing it. This emergent agency not only reworks the foreign-policy apparatus of each participating state (most especially the intelligence agencies), but also shapes foreign-policy formation itself, as the maintenance of the UKUSA infrastructure (listening posts, secret eavesdropping programs, etc.) becomes a priority for the entire foreign-policy apparatus. Further, it links processes of policy formation in ways that change the definition of the "national interest." In the next chapter I turn to another such harmonization of bureaucracies that shapes on the national interest, this time not in the world of intelligence, but in military defense.

THREE

Interoperability and Standardization in NATO

In December 1953 the governments of Belgium, Canada, France, the United Kingdom, and the United States announced their collective decision to adopt a standard .30 caliber (or 7.62mm) small-arms cartridge (see fig. 3.1). The announcement of a technical standard marked the end of a debate that had begun almost as soon as NATO formed, in 1949. In January 1951 Dwight Eisenhower (who would shortly become Supreme Allied Commander) reported from multiple allied capitals a "considerable confusion and frustration resulting from failure to reach decisions on . . . types of weapons to be manufactured. . . . Some expeditious solution in a number of specific instances is essential if we are to recreate national enthusiasm for an intensified defense effort."[1] From this telegram, it is clear that at stake was not only technical issues of standardization but also a sense of collective endeavor, an affective orientation among political and military elites toward a new future of collective security (in which an attack on one ally was considered an attack on all).

The debate over which bullet to use began in earnest in August 1951.[2] Despite comparative trials of various contenders, the decision was difficult as it was not solely about the properties of the ammunition (i.e., which was "best"), but also about a series of other considerations. First, hidden in the technical debate was a debate over the tactical training of soldiers in anticipation of future war. The British advocated their own .280 caliber cartridges, which had less power than the .30 caliber bullets of the French and Americans but made it easier to control

Figure 3.1 NATO standard .30 caliber (or 7.62mm) bullets. Photo by Jayel Aheram, used unaltered via a Creative Commons license (CC BY-SA 2.0).

fully automatic fire. The .30 caliber bullets had more power but were mainly intended for targeted fire of small bursts (table 3.1). Therefore, the selection of the bullet would also shape the ways in which soldiers' bodies were to be patterned through tactical training.[3] Second, the bullet question was necessarily connected to the geo- of geopolitics: the .280 bullet was lead-centered, and the Americans argued that they would not have enough lead to produce the British bullet during wartime if supplies from the Commonwealth were diverted for domestic war-fighting purposes. The British disputed this analysis, noting that only one-third of American lead came from the Commonwealth.[4] Third, and not for the last time, the United Kingdom was caught between its geopolitical self-perceptions as "the USA's bridge to Europe" and as the leader of the Commonwealth. Indeed, a separate process of Commonwealth military standardization was ongoing, with Australia, New Zealand, and Pakistan all prepared to adopt the British .280 standard. Britain's choice would ripple well outside of NATO.

While it was not the NATO nations' first decision to standardize, the matter of bullet selection was nevertheless crucial in that it was fundamental to much that followed. That this was a crucial first step helps to

TABLE 3.1 **Ballistic Details of T65 and .280 Ammunition**

	U.S. T65	U.K. .280
Bullet weight in grains	137	139
Velocity in feet per second at:		
Muzzle	2,770	2,530
400 yards	1,868	1,809
800 yards	1,134	1,280
1,200 yards	845	986
2,000 yards	640	767
Working pressure in tons per square inch	23.2	18.3
Mean radius at 600 yards (accuracy)	5.29"	3.2"
Wood penetration at:		
400 yards	21.1"	27.4"
1,200 yards	7.7"	13.2"
2,000 yards	.5"	2.9"
Penetration of steel helmet (max. range)	1,200 yards	800 yards
Recoil energy in foot lbs	11.0 plus	7.44
Weight of 100 rounds in lbs	5.19	4.50
Length of round in inches	2.8	2.54

Source: Technical Comparison of the .30 (T65) and .280 caliber bullets, prepared for the Prime Minister's Briefing, FO 371/96562, National Archives, London.

explain the willingness of the U.K. government to forego its own ammunition, already in production. Internal documents indicate that the British Foreign Office was prepared as early as October 1951 to concede the point and unleash future rounds of standardization.[5] First and foremost, the .30 caliber round opened the door to the standardization of the rifles that fired it. This standardization would remain incomplete, however; by 1957 the United Kingdom, Belgium, and Canada had all adopted the Belgian-made FN rifle, while the United States adopted its own T44, on the basis that its similarity to previous American rifles would ease the transition with regard to training (this presaged consistent ongoing tensions over the balance between European-made and American-made equipment within NATO).[6] Still, each rifle fired the standard NATO round, allowing for one allied state to resupply another regardless of what rifle they used. The continued disjuncture in rifles, however, unleashed yet another wave of objects to standardize: the clips and cartridges that hold the standard bullets. Where they could not be standardized, new adapters had to be designed to render the various rifles and bullets interoperable.

The example of the NATO standard round hints at some of the complexities of interoperability and standardization. The enmeshing of military assemblages over time requires not only the reterritorialization of these second-order bodies politic to include one another, but also requires the recoding of first-order bodies politic through continuous training. Further, as more-than-human assemblages they also require the design of various materials and procedures to mediate between them. Nor does this enmeshing occur in a void; the production of interoperability is always shaped by a wider array of force relations, such as the political economy of weapons production and the changing technologies of warfare. Crucially, the production of interoperability in NATO enables the circulation of certain affective orientations that help the politico-military assemblage cohere over time: confidence, enthusiasm, and a sense of collective agency. When progress toward interoperability is hampered, those feelings are replaced, as Eisenhower notes, by feelings of frustration and vulnerability. The affective orientation toward NATO collectivity is crucial not only because it underpins the doctrine of collective security, but also because it serves as the backdrop for the subsequent making of foreign policy by state elites.

In this chapter I first examine how the everyday diplomacy of interoperability is conducted, with an eye to the ways in which power and space shape this field. Then I proceed to examine the two areas in which NATO seeks to produce interoperability: procedures and materiel. Rather than argue that these two fields can be understood as proceeding inexorably toward an ideal state of harmonization, I note that progress in these fields is uneven precisely because of the differing material processes into which NATO seeks to intervene (embodied routines and weapons-system development) and because both fields are constantly buffeted by geopolitical and technological change. Therefore NATO's quest for interoperability resembles nothing so much as a satellite in orbit; it is constantly falling toward the earth without ever reaching it. I conclude with a discussion of the ways in which interoperability, beyond improving the capabilities of the NATO alliance to fight together, serves both as a peacetime attractor for other states and as a potential lever to use against them. By linking allied state apparatuses and marking off pariahs, interoperability serves as a military infrastructure of affect that shapes political subjectivities from the citizen-soldier to the president and prime minister.

Negotiating Interoperability
Conceptualizing Interoperability

"Interoperability refers to the ability of different military organizations to conduct joint operations. These organizations can be of different nationalities or different armed services (ground, naval and air forces) or both. Interoperability allows forces, units or systems to operate together. It requires them to share common doctrine and procedures, each other's infrastructure and bases, and to be able to communicate with each other."[7] This quote, from a 2006 NATO public-affairs document, defines interoperability simply as the ability of different military entities to work with one another toward a common end, specifying both embodied and technological dimensions as necessary. This is a textbook example of assemblage theory as articulated by Manuel DeLanda, who argued that "the components of an assemblage may be detached from it and plugged into a different assemblage in which its interactions are different."[8] That is to say, the elements—whether human or technological—that come together to form a national military have been designed with certain properties that, when entering into assemblage with other elements of that same national military, enable certain capacities to emerge: fighting coherently on a battlefield, engaging in at-sea rescue missions, and so on. However, when elements of that military assemblage are detached and enter into relation with another nation's military assemblage, those same capacities may not be reproduced. The properties of those elements must be engineered (through training or design) in order to produce the emergent effect of interoperability in a given context.

While military alliances are a long-standing feature of international relations, the rise of interoperability as a key concept in military circles is largely a result of geopolitical changes wrought during the twentieth century. First, the rise of the highly technical military forces that came to dominate armed conflict in the world wars unleashed a new drive toward innovation and specialization, both with regard to the equipment and the people who maintained and operated it. This territorialization of new weapons systems as discrete entities was effective in that it produced new military capacities (e.g., missions enabled by armored tanks, machine guns, fighter-bombers, and the people who made them work), but had the countervailing effect of undermining the coherence of the state's armed forces, especially between the branches of the military; for instance, land-based and sea-based planes were jealously maintained as separate systems by their respective armed services, often to the detriment of fighting effectiveness.[9] The second twentieth-century development that helped fuel the rise of interoperability was the rise of permanent military alliances. The era of fluid alliances—perhaps most clearly apparent in the idea of the "Concert of Europe" that dominated the long nineteenth century—foregrounded the need for militaries to be autochthonous and to keep secret their procedures, stockpiles, and capabilities, as any ally might eventually be a rival. However, the creation of the Cold War alliances shifted this logic, marking the ability of a multinational alliance to fight coherently together as an existential need. It was no longer enough to harmonize the technical practices of a state's military branches (not that there was great effort in this area either); they also had to be harmonized with those of other states. Given the strength of institutional cultures at each of those scales (e.g., the army or the state), such simultaneous reterritorialization would require intense commitment and diplomacy.

Indeed, diplomacy is key to maintaining this commitment, as a variety of dangers threaten the process: remaking the military infrastructure of a state is expensive, and must be laid alongside all the other competing claims for government funds. Further, remaking military infrastructure threatens the political coherence of some states (as marked by debates over European military-industrial capacity, declining sovereignty, and American dominance in NATO).[10] Finally, reterritorialization of national militaries is hard work, requiring huge amounts of bureaucratic effort and constant retraining of bodies enmeshed in the NATO assemblage. It can happen only so fast. Therefore, the production of interoperability is meant to be flexible and to occur through constant processes of negotiation that work toward consensus on where and how interoperability can be brought about. "Interoperability does not necessarily require common military equipment. What is important is that this equipment can share common facilities and is able to communicate with other equipment."[11] As the deputy director of the NATO Standardization Office put it, "We have a NATO policy that you can reach interoperability through many means. You want everyone to be able to fight in Afghanistan together. So first, I can standardize the weapons. Or, second, I procure the same weapons for everyone. Or third, everyone uses his or her own weapons but we train everyone to use everyone else's weapons. So standardization is but one avenue to interoperability."[12] Of course, the three routes outlined here are all standardizations of one kind or another: the weapons can be common to all, they can be interchangeable (as with NATO rifles and ammo), or the bodies of the soldiers can be patterned in standard ways for a greater array of weapons. The flexibility of the system enables constant pressure to be applied over the long term toward interoperability via a wide array of standardizations.

The Bureaucracy of Interoperability

NATO's efforts toward interoperability date to the founding of the alliance. The Committee for Standardization was in fact the second body created by the allies, after the Military Committee.[13] In 1951 the Military Agency for Standardization (MAS) was established in London.[14] It comprised three service boards (land, sea, and air), each originally with a representative from Canada, France, the United Kingdom, and the United States (the four "producer" states, Canada being a last-minute addition). The first director of MAS was appointed in 1955 in an effort to coordinate the production of interoperability between the service boards; interoperability is an issue not only *across* national militaries but also *within* them, leading to a multidimensional set of negotiations. In 1963 membership of the service boards was widened to include all NATO members as full participants.[15]

MAS was intended to accelerate the production of interoperability among the new allies, but it struggled at first. It did not monopolize its own subject matter, as a separate board, the Communications-Electronics Coordination Section, was responsible for standardization in the field of communications, and a range of other committees maintained their own influence over procedures and materiel within their orbits: intelligence, security, meteorology, and research and development. Given that MAS was intended to coordinate the overall standardization of NATO's procedures and materiel, these fields constituted significant gaps in its competency, and so its success was limited.

Early on, MAS was a victim of the protectionist institutional cultures it was seeking to integrate (e.g., the carving out of intelligence as a distinct sphere must be understood alongside the contemporary developments in UKUSA intelligence cooperation). Indeed, it is clear that while some allies sought to protect their own individual interests, other groups of countries favored greater interoperability, just not with members of NATO. At particular issue was the revelation of research and development, which was seen as too important to be divulged to all allies. (In particular, the Americans, British, and Canadians preferred to share among themselves rather than with all of NATO.) The terms of reference for MAS specify that "NATO-wide standardization and standardization by groups of countries within NATO are complementary. Attempts to achieve NATO-wide standardization should not be allowed to impede standardization by smaller groups of NATO countries; standardization by groups will often be possible when NATO-wide standardization is not."[16] Again, this demonstrates NATO's willingness to accept partial progress rather than none; equally it shows that interoperability need not involve the production of singularity, but rather the enmeshing of multiplicity.

A review of MAS in 1980 (known as the AC/308 review) turned a critical eye on the organization, noting several problems, including poor centralization, a lack of prioritization and strategy, and "the fragmented and overlapping points in the NATO machinery at which nations can exercise control."[17] The committee conducting the review attributed these flaws to the improvisation that had marked NATO's history: "At many occasions the tasking and responsibilities of organizational elements had been adapted to serve current problems, each single measure understandable in its own context. But over the years the sum of pragmatic changes has led to the point where it was assessed that NATO machinery is in need of review."[18] The nature of combat had change since the end of World War II, and the complexity of the military assemblage had intensified with new technologies, doctrines, and fields of potential combat: "Close and effective co-ordination of the many separate divisions and organizations which have dealings with standardization is becoming more difficult as the subject continues to grow and become increasingly complex."[19] The affective force of these changes rippled through the MAS staff, which could not keep up with the workload and suffered from low morale. "The workload in MAS has continued to increase throughout the past year. . . . Two word processors have now been installed in MAS to increase efficiency and output. However, the availability of conference rooms, interpreters and translation facilities are close to saturation point."[20] Indeed, the materialized form of MAS would itself be reorganized by the force of these changes.

A new material infrastructure—inspired by the development of computer networks—was proposed to give MAS a new role in coordinating the decentralized standardization activities occurring among NATO member states. The NATO Standardization Information System would not hold technical information itself (side-stepping issues of national security around research and development), but would "be the coordinating link between all interested parties, e.g., planners, engineers, logisticians, etc." and would enable long-term planning by NATO by enabling MAS to look for gaps in the alliance's interoperability.[21] This more relational approach to standardization hints at the way in which interoperability is not centrally about the elimination of difference among national militaries and the production of a monolithic transnational NATO military. Rather, it is about coordinating difference and making it manageable, organizing bodies and materials in ways that produce new capacities. Any ambitions of early interoperability enthusiasts to produce a frictionless space through which the militaries could be unified were eliminated by the AC/308 review.

While elements of this modernist approach remain, MAS was fundamentally transformed in the twilight years of the Cold War, and especially in the post–Cold War era. In the 1990s MAS was renamed the NATO Standardization Agency—in 2014, it became the NATO Standardization Office (NSO)—and came to function as it does now: both as a space of diplomatic encounter between representatives of national militaries, and as a database of various ongoing processes of standardization. Parts of this database were opened up to partners and even the general public starting in 1990.

Diplomacy within NATO: Standardization of Standardization

Unsurprisingly for an organization that attempts to standardize protocols across a large multinational assemblage, the NSO has established standard protocols through which standards are negotiated.[22] Diplomacy within the NSO takes two forms: bottom-up and top-down. Bottom-up diplomacy is launched from the operating theater. If NATO soldiers, sailors, or airmen encounter an obstacle to their interoperability in the field, they report the event to their superior officers, who pass it up the chain of command until it is addressed by one of the service boards within NSO. Given an explicit problem to solve, the representatives do so in a way that does not undermine other aspects of interoperability. About 95 percent of standards are produced through the process of bottom-up reporting.[23]

Top-down standards originate in NATO headquarters, and because they are somewhat disconnected from the everyday practices of the military, they occasionally misfire: "The top-down ones require a lot of imagination, and usually the [standard] is already there."[24] Still, the top-down process can address overarching or strategic needs for interoperability before the cost of a lack of interoperability is felt on the ground. Top-down processes also allow for prioritization. To produce interoperability requires substantial time, energy, and money, and in the post–Cold War world budgets are under stress: "From the year 2000, there was a different approach to standardization. Before 2000, it was bottom-up. In the Cold War a lot of effort was put in NATO because our big enemy was there and everyone was afraid. There was no limit on money or resources. . . . In the year 2000, NATO realized that bottom-up was fine but the risk was to lose priorities. A top-down approach allowed only important things to be standardized."[25] Hence, we see a reassertion of the need for central coordination rather than for pure self-organization within NATO, just as was argued in 1955, when the first director of MAS was appointed, and in 1980, when the AC/308 review was undertaken. Constant attention and adjustment are required to strike the correct balance between deterritorialization and reterritorialization.

Negotiating a new standard is not simple or quick. The NSO has about eighty working groups, each focused on a particular technology or field of practice.[26] The working groups are composed of technically proficient experts in their fields. When a topic is submitted to the NSO for standardization, whether via top-down or bottom-up processes, it is assigned to the relevant working group. Once assigned, a single member of the group drafts a standard, which is then circulated for comment by all the other members. This takes about three years.[27] Once everyone agrees to the standard, it moves from the working group to the service boards for final approval. Issues that are perceived to have an immediate impact on a member state's national security can be fast-tracked, which moves the issue to the front of the queue and "can shave a year or more off the process."[28] When lives are at stake, new standards can be produced within six months. The U.S. land representative for standardization argued that the process is quite efficient: "I used to think the three-year process was terrible. But in the U.S. to get a tire approved for a vehicle takes four years. So what we do here in two to three years is pretty good."[29] The multidimensional complexity of this undertaking means that negotiations within the NSO require a strong sense of collective purpose and solidarity.

Of course, such collective purpose and solidarity is not inherent to NATO; it must be fostered. Spatially, the embeddedness of the NSO within NATO's Brussels headquarters helps to foster the sense of collective purpose; national delegations to NATO are arrayed down hallways, with only an unimposing sign and perhaps a custom-made welcome mat marking off, for instance, the Belgian office from the British one down the hall. The cafeteria at lunchtime is a multinational space of conviviality in which a shared sense of purpose (and, perhaps, of burdens) emerges.[30] This is crucial to the production of standards given the intrinsic complexity of the process: "Everything in NATO is voluntary. Sometimes people agree . . . but say, 'I cannot implement it because of money, operational reasons, etc. I agree, but today I am not in a position to implement it.' You agree out of solidarity. . . . Only in a few cases—three or four—does a single objector hold it up."[31] Often, the period for implementing a new standard is allowed to be quite long (ten years, for instance) in order to produce agreement and ease the burden of implementation. The upfront cost of executing a standard, however, becomes a cost savings over time, which itself serves to produce an affective predisposition among policy makers toward deeper integration. This became apparent in a discussion I had with the deputy director of the NSO, Cesare Balducci:

> BALDUCCI: We standardize for two reasons—to be interoperable and to optimize resources. With less, they can be as effective as before. If you want to bring things to Afghanistan and you are using an American C-7, this means that you are able to place your containers in another nation's airplane and you don't have to use your small plane ten times.
>
> DITTMER: So once you are into standardization, it becomes very expensive to leave?
>
> BALDUCCI: Yes.[32]

Interoperability relies on a common affective orientation toward a future of collective endeavor among policy makers. This affective orientation requires maintenance and engineering to sustain.

Of course, there are limits to this affective push toward solidarity and harmonization, and power can be seen to flow in ways that occasionally enforce stratification between the national militaries. For instance, if a standard has been agreed on but has not been implemented by a particular national military, that military will be excluded from missions that depend on that standard. Therefore, the desire by policy makers to remain full and complete NATO partners (with all the sense of collective agency that entails) helps to affectively predispose them to be honest in their negotiations and to take seriously their commitments. This is an unevenly distributed lever of power, however, as (for instance) the exclusion of the United States from NATO operations would be almost unthinkable.

Standardization as Database/STANAG as Immutable Mobile

If the NSO can be conceptualized as a material space in which a specific form of technical diplomacy unfolds, it also can be considered through the lens of a different materiality. Recalling that the NSO was remade as a database in the wake of the AC/308 review, it is worth noting that NATO defines a "standard" as "*a document*, established by consensus and approved by a recognized Body that provides, for common and repeated use, rules, guidelines or characteristics for activities or their results, aimed at the achievement of the optimum degree of order in a given context."[33] The definition of a standard via its material form, and the NSO as a repository of that form, hints at how standardization as a process is undertaken through the circulation of what Bruno Latour would refer to as "immutable mobiles."[34]

Immutable mobiles, which convey standards across space with minimal distortion, are known within NATO as STANAGs (Standardization Agreements). A STANAG

- Is a stand-alone document, distinct from a standard, that covers one or several subject-related Allied standards;
- Shall indicate the required capability, and related interoperability/ standardization requirement(s) to be fulfilled by its implementation;

  . . .

- Shall be developed, sent for ratification, promulgated, and distributed in both official NATO languages;

- Should be prepared to ensure its largest distribution to potential users, i.e., without classification marking;
- Is formatted in accordance with reference 1.1.3.4;
- Is identified with a four-digit number, which is allocated by the NSA in accordance with reference 1.1.3.4.[35]

The first two elements of this definition deal with the content of a STANAG: one or several related standards, with information on what capabilities their implementation will enable. The latter four elements of the definition address the mobility of the STANAG: formatting and identification numbers to enable their location within the NSO database, and the limitation of striations within the space of circulation that might result from language or security classification. Therefore, it is clear that STANAGS, once negotiated and promulgated, are the circulating materials that produce a space in which military procedures and materiel are standardized in the effort to produce interoperability.

If the STANAG is intended to be the same for everyone, as a document it enables a range of possible outcomes with regard to standardization. NATO recognizes three levels of standardization: compatibility, interchangeability, and commonality. Compatibility refers to the ability of objects or procedures to be used together without "unacceptable interactions."[36] This lowest level of standardization hints at the logic of assemblage that underpins these processes; the aim here is merely to ensure that no disruptive affects emerge from within the politico-military assemblage of NATO. It is a negative form of interoperability: the mere avoidance of problems rather than the positive production of synergy. The next level of standardization is interchangeability, which refers to a protocol through which multiple objects or procedures are available for use, with each producing the same outcome. The final level of standardization is commonality, in which difference within these objects or procedures is absent, enabling a pure state of standardization. The production of interoperability can come about through any of these forms of standardization; but as each STANAG circulates, coded with one of these levels of standardization, it maintains a unique relationship to difference. Having discussed the ways in which standards are produced and circulated as STANAGS, I turn to the outcomes of these standardizations in two realms: procedures and materiel.

Standardization of Procedures

Much of the early headway in standardization occurred in the field of procedures. A 1954 brief written for the North Atlantic Council summarizes a state of affairs that continues to the present: "I do not propose to consider the question of the standardization of operational and administrative procedures, training publications, etc., which [has been] covered fully. . . . Progress is steady and satisfactory; but this is only to be expected as this form of standardization is generally not complicated by factors outside the military sphere."[37] The long history of military efforts to govern bodies through drilling, procedures, and hierarchical authority makes the implementation of new transnational procedures relatively easy. Further, there is consensus that standardization in "such subjects as tactics, techniques, organization, reports, forms, maps, charts, and military terminology" ought to be universal across all NATO members.[38]

Some early procedural standardizations were fundamental to everything that followed. For instance, two of the first standards to be adopted stipulated English and French proficiency levels: "Being able to communicate in a common language is a prerequisite for interoperability."[39] This kind of linguistic protocol enables everything from effective communication at the level of strategy formulation to the complete integration of multinational aircrews for the E-3A Airborne Early Warning and Control System.[40] Similarly, one of the NSO's jobs is to maintain standard glossaries: of terms and definitions related to standardization, of all NATO's abbreviations, and so on.[41] The glossary of abbreviations alone is 330 pages long. The standardization of abbreviations may seem trivial, but in an organization with two official languages, it is a crucial step to avoid misunderstandings.

The procedural realm of standardization is perhaps most fundamentally understood through STANAG 2116, negotiated in 1963: a new NATO code system for equivalent ranks.[42] This STANAG sought to establish a grid of ranks for each member state's army, navy, and air force, thereby establishing a transnational hierarchy of authority. This was not as simple as it might appear, given first that NATO militaries vary widely in how many ranks they have, and second that as with any ordinal numbering, the "distance" between any two ranks can be filled with an infinite number of subranks and permutations. For example, some countries have multiple varieties of lieutenant, and no country except the United States has warrant officers as a special class of ranks between officers and the enlisted. In short, each military's rank hierarchy had to be made legible within the system of every other member state's military. This achievement, once promulgated and disseminated to the field, has enabled clear chains of command to form across military hierarchies, coding military bodies in ways that stave off confusion.

The procedures that are standardized across NATO are usually less fundamental, with narrow application. For instance, STANAG 1412 establishes procedures for how to transfer litters from ship to ship or from ship to air. STANAG 4329 governs NATO standard barcode symbologies. STANAG 2551 sets out common regulations for the establishment and employment of medical radiological incident investigation teams. Despite the narrowness of each STANAG, the sheer number of them hints at the extent to which everyday military practices of everyone from the lowliest private to the five-star general are harmonized across the North Atlantic area (and of course in "out-of-area" military zones, such as Afghanistan).

Of course, the circulation of STANAGs across national contexts is insufficient to produce interoperability. These procedures must be somaticized through training and drills, as described by the deputy director of the NSO: "STANAGs have to be transported into national procedures, including training. . . . With air-to-air refueling, there is a manual for how to do it, and this is given to each pilot. He has to approach from a certain side, send radio signals of a certain kind, and so on. There are established hand signals to ensure flight safety. Materially, you understand, a soldier doesn't care about the materials of standardization, but he cares about the procedures."[43] Interoperability emerges not only through the circulation of the standards, but also from the internalization and performance of rote, embodied action: approaching the plane in a standard way, using standard hand signals, and so on.

As with any form of governmentality, military procedures are incomplete, and everyday resistances can bubble up from within the ranks. Still, the military—more than most institutions—has the capability to produce political subjects amenable to a range of embodied actions far removed from societal norms (e.g., the taking of human life).[44] Therefore, it is fruitful to think of STANAGs and their localizing translations into military manuals and training regimens as vectors for affect.

STANAGS enter into assemblage with various media and soldiers such that they orient bodies in common ways, rendering nationalized military bodies and equipment interoperable.

The affective power of STANAGS is all the more important given the choice by NATO leaders to maintain military training as a national prerogative. A 1951 U.K. Foreign Office memo outlined this decision: "It was felt that differences of equipment would limit standardization of techniques and methods in basic and advanced training. Standardization should be applied to the end product and nations should be free to adopt their own means and methods to accomplish it. The Americans were opposed to coordination of European and North American training."[45] The lines along which NATO would have standardized training might have included a greater emphasis on singularity in the production of interoperability. The NATO standard ammunition round is one such counterfactual; the given reason for the United States refusal to adopt the Belgian-made FN rifle (which Britain and others had adopted) was that the American-made T44 was an easier transition for American soldiers already trained on the M1 rifle.[46] Such examples hint at how "the key to progress in standardization in both the material and non-material fields lies in prior agreement on the standardization of tactical doctrine, organization and training."[47] As it happened, however, the continued decentralization of NATO military training served to buttress the acceptance of multiplicity within NATO.

This is not to say, however, that there were no relations between the training institutions of the various national militaries. In 1959 the secretary-general of the Western European Union (WEU) asked the British War Office about the extent to which harmonization was occurring among the Western powers. The War Office replied,

> We exchange directing staff officers with Canada, Australia, USA and France and have students on courses at the colleges of fifteen countries. They in turn send students to the Staff College Camberley and, in some cases, to the Imperial Defence College and Joint Services Staff College. . . . Our liaison with the French is particularly close. Frequent visits are exchanged between the directing staffs of Camberley and the French Staff College and the Commandants also visit each other periodically. . . . I attach great importance of a close liaison with the colleges of other countries and I am certain that it is being achieved.[48]

While it is unclear what exactly changed in terms of curriculum or methods of training as a result of these exchanges and liaisons, it seems likely that they had some material impact on the way in which the bodies of soldiers, sailors, and airmen were patterned. At minimum, these exchanges served to produce a group within each national military that had personal relationships with people in other NATO militaries. These could be maintained and developed over the course of a career, leading to transnational cohorts linked by the affective bonds of somatic training and camaraderie.

Standardization of Materiel

If syncing the temporalities of military careers thus proves helpful to the unfolding of NATO interoperability in the nonmaterial sphere, a similarly long-wave temporality can be observed in the realm of war materiel. War materiel is fundamentally harder to standardize than procedures, as "difficulties arise from the national differences of industrial methods and production, the diversity of existing equipment, [and] the impracticability of immediately replacing the present equipment by new and standard equipment."[49]

The field of war materiel is one in which the cycle of design, production, and weapon lifespan can be measured in decades; to intervene in this field for the purposes of standardization requires the production cycles of producer nations to be synchronized, or at least brought into relation with one another. As a U.K. Ministry of Defence memo indicates, this is no easy task: "One of the real problems is that NATO member countries, either individually or collectively, are very much concerned with getting new equipment into service and have much less time to devote to the much more abstract problem of tactical concepts for equipment which might not come into service for twenty years, either directly as the result of long development and production cycles, or because of a re-equipment time-scale dictated by short-term plans."[50] Any top-down effort to wrench these processes into alignment would run up against so many political and economic interests as to be doomed; therefore, in 1954, NATO identified two parallel tracks through which to try to bring about interoperability in war materiel. For already existing equipment, priority would be given, in this order, to: "a) The standardization of components. b) The standardization of stores which are consumed in large quantities. c) The interchangeability of ammunition. d) The development of adaptors."[51] As with the NATO standard round, innovations like these enabled interoperability without necessarily intervening deeply into the production process for "end-item" materiel. Not until 1963 did the NATO Standing Group for Standardization openly discuss whether it was time for MAS to shift its attention from the development of adaptors to standard fittings (e.g., a standard fuel nozzle for aviation fuel) for equipment currently in development.[52] This gives some sense of the glacial temporality at which change in this sphere is intelligible.

But nibbling away at the edges of interoperability through adaptors was initially understood as a short-term tactic. One effort to produce more substantial standardization of equipment involved conducting comparative trials through which competing designs could be pitted against one another. This kind of intervention, however, could only be done early in the production cycle—for instance, at the prototype stage. This required an effort to identify opportunities when various production cycles might be hitched to one another.

NATO's International Staff proposed comparative trials in the early 1950s as a way of reducing the variety of equipment being produced in Europe, and also of achieving a more liberal weapons market: "The Continental countries consider that NATO Comparative Trials might lead to a reduction in types of equipment, thereby increasing standardization. They consider that the trials would have the effect of improving the standard of NATO equipment and that they would assist non-producer countries in placing orders for new equipment."[53] The attempt to deploy scientific metrics in an attempt to depoliticize and universalize questions of military production and produce a market in which the non-producer states might make rational decisions was predicated on the idea that "merit" would emerge apolitically from the comparative trials. The International Staff imagined MAS as the actor best positioned to depoliticize standardization through comparative trials, but MAS—aware of its role as a diplomatic space of encounter for the member states— resisted efforts to assign it this role. They did so by contesting the notion that merit could be attributed to equipment through comparative trials. According to a 1953 MAS report, "MAS could do no more than prepare a tabulation of the results of comparative trials. The MAS could not place the equipment tested in order of merit."[54] Given that the producer countries could provide quantitative data on their weapons' performance to interested parties, MAS argued that there was therefore little need for comparative trials. It was left to the nonproducer countries to argue that this data might overstate performance (an uncomfortable argument to make given the producer countries also tended to be the sine qua non of European collective security). In the end, Canada, Britain, and the United States carried the argument with a blunt statement of the innately political nature of war materiel production.

> They [the United States, the United Kingdom, and Canada] maintain that producer nations will not voluntarily accept decisions which would require them:
> a) To scrap equipment or cease production as the result of NATO trials.
> b) Accept equipment which, although it may represent a NATO choice, may not be suited to their particular needs, bearing in mind their wide commitments including those outside NATO.[55]

If the varying temporalities of weapons production were a crucial obstacle in the effort to produce interoperability, so were the imagined geographies of military action, which combined the imagined Soviet threat in Europe with the (neo)colonial aims of the United States, Britain, and France: "Some of these countries must of necessity use equipment designed to meet world-wide commitments; others need equipment suitable for a particular type of terrain or climate only. Therefore complete standardization of all items of military equipment throughout NATO is not practical."[56] As early as 1954, then, it was clear that the production of war materiel could not be standardized in the same fashion as procedures were. Where the aspiration of creating universal standards throughout NATO could be more or less realized in the realm of procedures, it could not be realized in the world of war materiel. In the matter of weaponry, merit was not a universal that could be derived from a metric rationalization. Rather, it depended on the context in which the weapons might be used; weapons meritorious for fighting on the plains of northern Europe might not be equally so in the rainforests of Southeast Asia. Perhaps even more crucially, merit emerged not only from metric testing, but also from the political and economic systems in which that testing was embedded (a state-based capitalism in which government spending buttressed the national economy). A 1977 memo from the U.K. Ministry of Defence makes this clear: "If standardization means the use of common equipment produced to exactly the same detailed specification then the pitfall of adopting the vast majority of US designed equipment is obvious and the effect on European high technology industries would be very serious."[57]

For these reasons, NATO abandoned comparative trials (and the universalism they embodied) in favor of a more relational approach. It decided that because standardization was voluntary, comparative trials would be of value only when standardization was vital and where progress necessitated such trials. Outside of these circumstances, regional groups that could cohere around certain criteria of judgment were encouraged to conduct their own trials.

The coalescence of these regional groups was encouraged by the creation of the Conference of National Armaments Directors (CNAD), in 1966. This venue provided a forum, parallel to MAS, in which "two or three countries get together because they have common interests in satisfying an operational requirement in broadly the same timescale and can each bring to the project a reasonable level of technological competence."[58] Through these shifting coalitions, overall NATO standardization would hopefully emerge within the realm of war materiel.

The oldest regional grouping of this sort actually predates NATO entirely. The so-called ABC group (America, Britain, and Canada) dates back to a May 1947 agreement on a general principle on standardization.[59] This group maintained and prioritized its own activities over the wider collaboration of NATO. The willingness of these NATO member states to share research and development information with one another far eclipsed their willingness to do so within MAS, and indeed ABC standardization was kept secret from NATO allies until 1952. Consequently, the French and Italians tended to view ABC standardization as an Anglophone conspiracy to control NATO policy.[60] Other countries simply felt caught in the middle. For instance, in 1956 the Dutch ambassador to the United Kingdom complained that ABC fears regarding the inadequacy of French counterintelligence had brought MAS work to a standstill. The U.K.'s Ministry of Defence recognized that "ABC security requirements have placed certain limitations on the work and in particular restricted the ability of the Agency to achieve standardization of actual equipment."[61] Therefore, the polycentric, stuttering progress of NATO standardization is both indebted to, and cursed by, the uneven affective intensities of trust within the alliance. The particular shape of NATO interoperability in the field of war materiel was generated by a productive imbalance of trust, which allowed smaller-scale collaboration where larger-scale collaboration might not have been possible, potentially enabling those collaborations to scale up within NATO.

It is, however, impossible to claim that ABC collaboration is an Anglophone "stitch-up," as other regional groupings have also been productive under the umbrella of CNAD. The Group of Four, for instance, included France, the United States, Britain, and West Germany. In the 1960s and 1970s, these countries' armaments directors met every six months, with their assistants meeting every three months. "The group exchanges information on respective armaments projects with a view to possibly eliminating one or another national programme, in favour of the adoption of a common solution, and with a view to coordinating the initiatives which are presented by the four countries at CNAD. This Group of Four is reported to have worked very successfully up to now [1975], notably because of its informal nature."[62] Regional groupings (either formal or informal) function as a complex Venn diagram of relations through which interoperability of end-items can (but need not) emerge.

If standardization of war materiel appears to involve more rational balancing of interests than is apparent in the standardization of procedures, this is because it undoubtedly does so. Overcoming the affective force of large-scale political-industrial processes such as the development cycle of weapons systems is a greater challenge than overcoming the relatively short-term cycles of military procedures and training harnessed in the standardization of procedures. Still, the impact of becoming enmeshed in these processes of war-materiel standardization undoubtedly changed the basis on which "rational" decision-making was made. First, the difficulty of producing standards in this field itself affected the ways in which producer nations thought of their own weapons systems. For instance, in 1978 the U.K. Ministry of Defence bragged, "Nationally, we place every item of the Army's equipment into one of twelve 'capability' fields, and keep our tactical concepts and capabilities in these fields under constant review. . . . This educated involvement in the concept field has had a real degree of influence on US and German thought."[63] In other words, the conceptual field of weapons development itself was made transnational through the involvement of these NATO members in processes of standardization.

Second, interoperability and standardization were understood in the late twentieth century as a response to the increasing cost of military defense: "The inescapable fact is that the increasingly sophisticated and high technology systems of today will cost more, and continue to cost more, than the systems they replace. And, to the extent to which standardization implies more cost-effective procurement, it adds, of course, to the Alliance's military resources."[64] Of course, if interoperability is understood as shaping the political subjects involved in it, then it becomes clear that instead of thinking of the increasing sophistication of modern warfare as driving greater and deeper interoperability as a form of cost savings, it is equally possible to imagine greater interoperability as *enabling* the development of more sophisticated weapons systems. Weapons systems are emerging alongside and within the NATO context, with causation not easily attributed to any single process but rather emerging out of their being inextricably mangled together. The more technologically sophisticated weapons of late modern warfare cross over the horizon of possibility only because of the increasingly transnational economies of scale that interoperability produces.

Power, Interoperability, and Political Subjects

Interoperability—in both its embodied and material-technological forms—works to remake political subjectivities, from the everyday soldier to the policy maker. While NATO and U.K. documents rarely acknowledge this process, it occasionally peeks into view. For instance, in 1979 the U.S. House Armed Services Subcommittee on NATO Standardization, Interoperability, and Readiness issued the Daniel Report, which sharply criticized many efforts to produce interoperability within NATO, arguing that the advantages were overstated and that the transnational coordination of military industries was a hindrance to both a competitive weapons market and to military readiness.[65] Implicit in this critique was a fairly narrow view that American weapons would be both more competitive in a "free market" and more effective; at the time, NATO's "two-way-street" policy, which required a relative balance of American and European weapons systems to be adopted by NATO, effectively subsidized "uncompetitive" European arms industries. Internally, the U.K. Ministry of Defence was highly critical of the Daniel Report, both critiquing its narrow economism and highlighting the *process* of building interoperability itself as contributing to the production of new political subjectivities: "I was disappointed that so little account was taken of the efforts made in Europe collectively to work together and, with the greatest respect to the Sub Committee, I felt that too much account was taken of the somewhat theoretical benefit of competition in this market."[66] The official response combined the two critiques: "Benefits in effectiveness [resulting both from a lack of duplication in R&D and from overall savings] are likely to be accompanied by greater political cohesion."[67] The interweaving of NATO's militaries through interoperability creates a virtuous circle that appears both economically and militarily rational, even as it rewires the political cognition of those making the decision.

However, the development of these new subjectivities through interoperability is not an entirely homogenizing process; it is uneven in its intensity and direction. A 2014 unclassified NATO PowerPoint claims that "doctrine, standardization, and interoperability is the DNA of NATO."[68] This is an apt phrase, as DeLanda notes that DNA is an example of how assemblages can be coded in nondiscursive ways.[69] Thus, interoperability is not just about the territorialization of NATO as a politico-military assemblage ("political cohesion") but also about the way in which that assemblage is coded. It is for this latter reason—and its interrelation with the economics of weapons production—that interoperability has been so contested (for instance by the Daniel Report).

At NATO Headquarters in suburban Brussels all the member states' flags fly at the same height, but this is not a true reflection of the power relations within the organization, in which the United States generally occupies a privileged role. There is a reason that that two-way-street concept was contested from within the United States but not from within Europe; in fact, the Daniel Report justified its criticism of the two-way-street policy by arguing that if the massive U.S. spending on maintaining military personnel in Europe were laid alongside European purchases of American war materiel, a rough balance of payments within NATO already existed. Therefore, the actual standards produced within the NSO must themselves be understood not only as a way of weaving together the member states of NATO, but also as a lever of power for shaping NATO in particular ways. As the U.S. representative to the NSO Land Board argued, this was particularly useful to the United States.

> If we wanted to pay for all this ourselves, educate every country on what we do and get them to adopt our standards, to achieve interoperability? It would cost a fortune. . . . We influence how other nations act or react while involved in NATO-led initiatives. It is a tool

for leadership. . . . The U.S. is the custodian of about 60 percent of NATO standards and the reason is because the U.S. is the energy and manpower behind a lot of the efforts.[70]

This influence is of course not the same thing as "Americanization"; rather than a unidirectional radiating of power, the role of the U.S. in NATO is a more nuanced and relational hegemony.[71] Crucially, the borders of NATO itself do not limit this hegemony.

The end of the Cold War initiated a rethinking of the role of interoperability and standardization within NATO. To the extent that NATO had territorialized itself as a coherent more-than-human assemblage, with a sharp boundary between inside and outside with regard to procedures and war materiel, this territorial framing was called into question, as this sharp boundary could also be understood as a geographical limit to NATO's power. The subsequent declassification of most STANAGs worked to dissolve the limit to the geographic context in which NATO could easily operate: "The range of possibilities for NATO is endless. We can go somewhere for natural disaster, peacekeeping, peace enforcement, or war. And when we go, we go with a lot of partners who are not in NATO. We need to be interoperable with as much of the world as possible."[72] A few topics remain private, such as in the fields of intelligence cooperation and nuclear weapons. Otherwise, however, STANAG security classifications are as minimal as possible so that they might circulate far and wide, shaping practices well beyond NATO. Thirteen thousand people are registered with the NSO's protected website, from which there are six hundred downloads per day. "People are doing this because they [STANAGs] are very important to all these people. They are not fun to read. We have forums as well, online, in which people discuss the STANAGs as they are developed."[73]

The development of interoperability was explicitly wielded as a political tool by NATO in the wake of the Cold War through the development of the Partnership for Peace, the NATO-Russia Council, the Mediterranean Dialogue, and the Istanbul Cooperation Initiative.[74] These efforts aim to reshape the political cognition of elites and military personnel (usually from states near NATO's territory) by enmeshing them in the affective field of NATO's interoperability through participation in everything from military exercises to actual NATO missions, from Bosnia-Herzegovina (Russia, Egypt, United Arab Emirates) to Afghanistan (Australia, New Zealand). In other ways, circulation of STANAGs accrues advantage to NATO members. In some cases it fosters a pragmatic orientation toward thrift; for instance, the UN adopted NATO's standards for demining, as "having two different procedures was a big waste. By sharing standards member states all benefit because we are paying for the UN, we are paying for it all."[75] More crassly, if other countries adopt NATO standards it becomes easier to sell weapons to them. Finally, interoperability is a lever for reshaping political subjectivities. Balducci, of the NSO, described a diplomatic trip: "Recently I was in Tbilisi to help them set up their national standardization agency. They want to get into NATO. We were doing the same thing in Ukraine until recently [the 2014 Russian intervention]. It [interoperability] is great for making friends because it is technical, not seemingly political."[76] "Seemingly" is crucial here; practitioners of interoperability clearly understand it to be a form of *puissance*, or constitutive power.

Beyond simply being an attractive force that subtly shapes the world in NATO's image, the centrality of NATO in the world of standards offers possibilities for direct action (*pouvoir*, or actualized power). For example, non-NATO states have long adopted the NATO Codification System, which was an unclassified standard system for cataloging defense equipment. In 1968 Britain "weaponized" the system by refusing to release the codes for equipment that was subject to the South African embargo, so that South Africa would have more difficulty in obtaining alternative suppliers in non-embargo states. Cornelious Doraton made a similar argument in a contemporary context: "The quickest way to strangle a country is to embargo the standard procedures through which that country's banks interact with the world. The same goes for natural resources, which are bought and sold in dollars. So if you don't have the ability to do funding transfers, you're done. A lot of the levers that can be pulled by policy makers exist because of standardization."[77] Such technicalities rarely make the news, but have featured prominently in recent measures deployed against Russia in the wake of the Crimean invasion.

The production of interoperability and standardization in NATO is a complex intervention into the fields of both military procedures and war materiel. Through this a range of political subjects are remade—from the lowest ranks to the most eminent policy makers—and this both reterritorializes NATO itself as an assemblage and functions as an affective attractor for other states that are formally outside the North Atlantic

Alliance. Those state elites participating in processes of interoperability see their own agency enhanced through the new lines of flight that open up their militaries to capabilities of collective action, but at the same time uneven power relations are generated through the varying affective intensities produced by the politico-military processes unfolding at varying temporalities. While it is easy to focus on interoperability and standardization as a mechanism for generating American, British, and French arms sales, or as a switch to be flipped in economic warfare with Russia, I have emphasized the integrative power—or puissance—of interoperability, which has proven so powerful that NATO has outlived its ostensible nemesis (the Soviet Union) by over twenty-five years. Indeed, if the end of the Cold War unleashed a new wave of globalization, interoperability and standardization might be understood as the clearest embodied and material manifestation of that globalization in the technical-military field.

FOUR

Assembling a Common Foreign
and Security Policy

As I walked up the Rue de la Loi in Brussels, I knew something was wrong. The police were stringing barbed wire across the street, and a group of protesters on the island in the Schuman roundabout were being moved on. I had come to Brussels to interview staff involved with producing the European Union's Common Foreign and Security Policy (CFSP). I turned to one of the café-dwellers sitting outside right where the barbed wire was being put up: "What's going on?" "There is an emergency Council [of Ministers] meeting on Ukraine," he replied. A light bulb flashed in my head: much of the news I had been watching in my hotel room about the Russian invasion of Crimea—the debates, the schisms within Europe, the back-channel diplomacy—was unfolding within a block or two of where I stood, in the glassy modern buildings of the European Quarter. It had not occurred to me until now that my research itinerary might actually be interrupted by current events as they rippled through the normal routines of Brussels life.

Fully expecting my first interviewee, who worked in a crucial role within the European External Action Service (EEAS), to now be unavailable, I waited until the designated time in the café, watching police unfurl the material infrastructure of security. Anticipation was in the air as the EU prepared to receive its member states' presidents and prime ministers for a high level meeting of its Council. At the appointed time, I arrived at the EEAS headquarters and, after clearing security, I was sent up. "I'm so grateful you can fit me in on such a busy day," I offered as a preemptive apology for taking up my interviewee's time. "To be honest, I'm surprised you're still seeing me." He smiled kindly in return and replied, "Oh, the preparation for this was done yesterday. Today I'm doing staff appraisals. This is a welcome break."

The contrast between the outside and the inside of the EEAS offices, between the pomp and anticipation in the streets and the quiet and boredom inside, was startling. While the presidents and prime ministers were sitting in the Council chambers deciding the fate of nations, the staff that managed the day-to-day diplomacy of the EU were engaged in human resources instead of in CFSP. It was my first introduction to the complex interrelations among the spaces and times in which European foreign policy is produced. The connections and disconnections between the national capitals, Brussels, and the various embassies and representations in third countries produce a fluid and constantly changing relational space in which power and authority are both embedded and emergent.

Even as it appeared that the leaders of the member states had arrived in Brussels to decide EU foreign policy, they were doing so in a context in which EU foreign policy was already—in a range of ways—embedded within their own foreign-policy apparatuses. Like a Möbius strip, in which the outside is also the inside, the European Common Foreign and Security Policy is both constituted by the member states and yet also an existing context that shapes their own processes of policy making. Rather than adopting the institutionalist approaches that dominate EU studies, I primarily focus on the engineering of space and time that contributes to the production of consensus within the everyday diplomacy of the CFSP. If in chapter 1 I laid out a materialist take on traditional diplomacy that contributes to understanding of the various infrastructures and atmospheres in London that underpinned British foreign-policy formation, in this chapter I return to traditional diplomacy but do so with a decentered, transnational approach. While London continues to feature, it does so as an exemplar of processes occurring in member states rather than as a "canary in the coalmine" at the forefront of changes occurring in the wider diplomatic system.

Considering the CFSP as the emergent effect of a complex and evolving assemblage of foreign-policy apparatuses is a fruitful way to consider the topic, as it enables both a microscaled temporal analysis centered on the embodied aspects of diplomacy and the inculcation of trust and new subjectivities, as well as a more macroscaled temporal analysis that considers the way in which the foreign-policy apparatuses—EU foreign ministries, member state representatives to Brussels, European delegations and EU member embassies in third countries, the European Commission and European External Action Service—are all synchronically emerging with and through one another.[1] That the day-to-day practices of producing CFSP should also affect the workings in national capitals—and vice versa—is contrary to the commonsense understanding of EU foreign policy (if such a thing as "commonsense understanding of EU foreign policy" can be said to exist).

I begin with a genealogy of the European CFSP. As with intelligence cooperation, CFSP has both a clear origin point and historical antecedents that helped shape that official, institutional origin. As these antecedents are crucial to the eventual workings of CFSP, I map them in some detail. I then turn to the spatialities in which CFSP is negotiated in an everyday sense. I emphasize the ways in which a complex array of actors is brought together in a relational space of affects—both via technology and in face-to-face situations—to bring about consensus on a unified foreign policy. Following this, I turn to the engineering of temporalities in London and Brussels. Foreign policy formation in an everyday sense is profoundly structured by rhythms that must be coordinated in order to exercise power both within Brussels and beyond. Of course, these rhythms are frequently disrupted by crises and therefore improvisation is needed. I conclude by returning to the twin theorizations of power found in each case study—*puissance* and *pouvoir*—to discuss CFSP with regard to what it does for and to the EU, as well as for and to the member states. Through all this, I show the ways in which affects, procedures, and materials are deployed in a knowing fashion by foreign-policy actors in the EU and in the member states to make some courses of action more likely than others. This is true not only in terms of specific foreign policies, but also with regard to whether any kind of foreign policy at all emerges from the complex assemblage of CFSP. As critics of European foreign policy have frequently noted, this is always a danger lurking in the background of such matters.

Evolution of Political Cooperation in Europe

The CFSP has antecedents in the late 1950s, when the formation of the European Community (EC) first offered the potential for a European foreign policy. Several early abortive attempts seemed to indicate the limited potentialities of the EC for collective foreign policy. Still, as negotiations over the creation of the Common Market and the Economic and Monetary Union bore fruit in the late 1960s, a positive affective orientation to the future—optimism—returned to European leaders. In 1969 foreign ministers at the Hague Summit were asked to investigate the best way to produce political unity, leading to an agreement that paved the way for the establishment of the European Political Cooperation, in 1970. In this agreement, known as the Luxembourg Report, the ministers committed themselves politically to the exchange of information, which would aid a harmonization of views and a strengthening of solidarity, and potentially joint action.[2] Parallels with the development of intelligence cooperation and collective security in NATO in terms of pouvoir and puissance are evident even at this early point, and it is worthwhile remembering that European Political Cooperation was taking place concurrently with the intensification of UKUSA cooperation and NATO interoperability (albeit with the latter two processes including non-European countries).

The time and context for the Luxembourg Report is significant, as it overlapped with Charles de Gaulle's withdrawal of French military forces from the unified NATO command and his subsequent efforts to lead a European bloc free of American influence and dominated by France. Being dependent on the United States for defense from the Soviet Union, West Germany, in particular, dragged its heels on de Gaulle's plan; indeed, in order to proceed with Political Cooperation the European bloc made a tacit agreement (not to be found in the text of the Luxembourg Report) to exclude any security or defense discussions that infringed on NATO.[3] The vaguely anti-American slant to Political Cooperation ended in 1973, when the United Kingdom joined the EC, as its particular take on Atlanticism differed from de Gaulle's.

By the time the United Kingdom joined the EC, Political Cooperation had become fairly institutionalized, but was without institutions.

> In a way Political Cooperation was a means of having cooperation in foreign policy without engaging in any of the institutional stuff. . . . Basically the Council of Ministers meeting of the European Community met in Brussels, and then they would go off to the capital of the community country that held the [rotating] presidency to hold foreign policy meetings. The British were among the first to say this was stupid

and we could just continue meeting in Brussels without there being any compromise on what was Community competence and what wasn't.[4]

Despite the United Kingdom's reputation for opposing a coordinated European foreign policy, no less a figure than Margaret Thatcher made a strong case for improved Political Cooperation. In 1984 a pamphlet titled *We Are the Future* was published in her name; this was followed by a formal document that introduced "sensible kinds of propositions for trying to get more coherent policy making."[5]

There was good cause for the United Kingdom to be interested in Political Cooperation, both then and in 1973. Of the nine participants at the time of the United Kingdom's accession, only France and the United Kingdom had a "global" foreign policy. Today the "global" aspirations of EU members are slightly more muddled.

> The Germans were—still are—very reticent for obvious reasons, and all others weren't players really and still aren't. I mean, you've got countries like Poland and Spain and to a lesser extent Italy who want to be power players, but the rest don't really. I mean, that's why—if you take the Iranian nuclear policy—basically the policies are made by three nation-states independent of the European Union and that becomes the EU policy and everyone else signs up to it.[6]

For Britain and France, Political Cooperation offered a chance to magnify their own power—as in pouvoir—without having to actually compromise with many other nations. But how did Political Cooperation actually unfold in the pre-CFSP era?

The early years of Political Cooperation were marked by the relative infrequency of ministerial meetings—no more than twice a year. Originally, political directors met four times a year, which doubled in 1972, to eight times a year. Working groups formed on topics of perennial interest, such as the Middle East, in order to advance planning between ministerial meetings. Further ad hoc meetings of analysts occurred where opportune, such as in anticipation of a United Nations General Assembly. In 1973 (when West Germany became a member of the UN) the nine EC countries cast almost 47 percent of their votes together in the General Assembly. By 1974, that number had risen to nearly 61 percent, where it more or less remained.[7] A central fact of Political Cooperation was its informality. There was no secretariat outside of the Council of

Ministers presidency, so there was no independent institutional fol-
low-up between meetings. Rather, the ministers would go into a meeting room and emerge with a decision about what to do, which would
then be communicated to their national capitals. This informal process
"wasn't unorganized—it just didn't have a Brussels-based structure."[8]
After a meeting, if there was a text to be agreed on, the dialogue would
continue via telegram between the capitals. Some landmark decisions
came out of this process, such as coordinated European leadership in
the creation of the Conference on Security and Cooperation in Europe
(CSCE), which is now the Organization for Security and Cooperation in
Europe (OSCE). However, Political Cooperation outcomes would quite
often be disconnected from EC policy, which had competency for trade
and aid. Therefore, various levers of foreign policy were held by different
decision-making bodies, and they sometimes worked at cross-purposes.
This makes sense; Political Cooperation was an improvised attempt to
use the occasion of EC meetings to do things for which the EC did not
have competency. The bureaucratic disjuncture between the EC institutions and these extra-institutional negotiations served to stifle the necessary procedural interactions that might produce coherence (it was
only after U.K. accession that it was deemed unnecessary to travel to
another city in order to have foreign-policy discussions).

Diplomats at the time perceived that Political Cooperation had
peaked in the late 1970s, as divisive issues such as the fate of Palestine or
South African apartheid came to dominate the agenda in the late 1970s
and early 1980s. In order to reassemble Political Cooperation, some
minor amendments were offered to improve cohesion. For instance,
representatives of the EC were given permission to attend ministerial
meetings, a practice that theretofore had been staunchly blocked by the
French. Small gestures such as this—as well as the eventual inclusion of
Greece, Spain, and Portugal in Political Cooperation meetings (prior to
their eventual accession)—contributed to a new, outward-looking EC
that was (temporarily at least) not consumed with internal reform.

The London Report of 1981 established a new set of expectations
intended to make Political Cooperation work under crisis conditions.
If three member states were to request it, an emergency meeting of
ministers or political directors (in Brussels) or of EC ambassadors (in
a third country) could be called within two days. While these crisis meetings did not guarantee a cohesive response or even a collective decision,

they did embed a temporal expectation—that the member states would work together even under emergency conditions.[9] There was also a broadening of the Political Cooperation assemblage, with deeper relations forged between the EC states and the various tools at their disposal—whether those in the European Commission (trade and aid) or in the arsenals of the member states (military might). As a result of these new links, member states were more likely to collectively sanction a third country economically or diplomatically or, alternatively, to constructively engage with a third state or a region. As Elfriede Regelsberger notes, "The fact that EPC [European Political Cooperation] texts in the 1980s have included 'footnotes' from one or more governments explaining individual positions could also be seen as a positive sign: the increasingly advanced character of EPC naturally impinges more often and more directly on (and collides with) specific foreign policy interests of the member states."[10] Perhaps, after all, it was time to formalize Political Cooperation.

The broader troubles of the European Community added to pressures for reform. In the early 1980s massive schisms over the EC budget, the Common Agricultural Policy, and other headline issues hampered Political Cooperation in its current form, giving new impetus to changing the member states' obligation from a political to a legal commitment. The long process of EC reform culminated in the signing of the Single European Act (1986), which formalized Political Cooperation (see Title III, Article 30). Crucially, in doing so, it brought Political Cooperation into the treaty structure underpinning the European project; Political Cooperation was materialized in the form of a secretariat. Notably, the Single European Act maintained the distinction between Political Cooperation and defense cooperation. As a wave of reforms unfolded in the 1990s, however, this distinction would dissolve and CFSP would be born.

The Maastricht Treaty was the crucial turning point at which Political Cooperation became the Common Foreign and Security Policy.[11] Maintaining both France's and Britain's concerns over national competency in foreign affairs led to the construction of three "pillars" within the EU, each with different decision-making procedures. The CFSP was included in the second pillar, and after the 1997 Treaty of Amsterdam, a new post of high representative for CFSP was created. Decision-making within the CFSP remained resolutely intergovernmental, as it had been under

Political Cooperation; representatives of the European Commission were allowed to attend, but only as associates. The regular meetings of political directors that had occurred under Political Cooperation were replaced by the new Political and Security Committee, which remains responsible for daily management of CFSP to this day. The rotating six-month presidency of the member states continued in this structure as well.

A final twist in the story of the creation of today's CFSP comes from the Lisbon Treaty, which abolished the pillar system and aimed "to provide a political superstructure to the European Union's undoubted international economic power base."[12] The treaty's creation of the EEAS outside of existing structures such as the European Commission or the Foreign Affairs Council upended the old CFSP order and renewed some member states' concerns over competency;[13] however, the treaty's replacement of the six-month rotating Foreign Affairs Council presidency with the high representative as chair of meetings provided much-needed continuity in terms of European foreign-policy agendas.[14] Further, the formation of the EEAS has created a vast worldwide network of European delegations to states outside of Europe that either coexist with EU member states' embassies or—as has often become the case—have come to stand in for a national diplomatic presence. This network has broadened the relational space of CFSP; foreign-policy coordination must now take place in Brussels, as well as in third-party capitals, where any array of EEAS and national representations coexist. The relatively institutionalist history outlined in this section is therefore insufficient to describe how consensus is produced throughout this complex assemblage, and therefore I now turn to the engineering of affects within various sites in this relational space.

Negotiating CFSP

Just as intelligence cooperation and the development of NATO interoperability had both bottom-up processes of self-organization and top-down processes of hierarchical control operating at the same time, with frequent attempts at rebalancing, the creation of the EEAS can be understood as an attempt to impose hierarchy (and therefore coherence) in a field that had been (intentionally) disorganized and improvisational. While the long-term effects of the creation of the EEAS will not be known for some time, it is clearly a new actor in the already complex system through which the CFSP is forged. Other actors include the European Commission, the individual member states, and of course various non-governmental organizations or think tanks that are related to—but not part of—the European Union.[15] The circulation of people, documents, and affects through this complex relational space needs to be traced to understand not only how specific policies emerge, but how any policies emerge at all given the various competing interests.

Ultimately, CFSP is the responsibility of the Foreign Affairs Council (which meets monthly), but the day-to-day handling of CFSP is delegated to the Political and Security Committee (PSC). The committee's work is highly routinized, with two meetings a week, on Tuesdays and Thursdays, although during a crisis, the committee can meet every day. On Friday afternoon, EEAS distributes a draft agenda for the Tuesday meeting, based on what work is developed well enough to be debated by the committee. On Monday morning, at 10 a.m., the committee holds an internal meeting with the chair to review the briefings prepared. At 10:30 a.m., the desk officers who prepared the briefings are quizzed on the various issues that they have put forward, the status of negotiations among the twenty-eight member states on those issues, and so on. The fundamental purpose of this meeting is to confirm a fair amount of preexisting (if incomplete) consensus around the issues to be raised. By 11 a.m., the committee circulates a set of draft conclusions to the member states. The 2 p.m. meeting of the so-called Nicolaidis Group is the first meeting at which member states' ambassadors are present. If any of the member states raise concerns, the EEAS staff meet again at 5 p.m. to work on achieving consensus (or deciding to drop an issue for the time being). "So the aim is . . . if the preparation has gone well, by the time we have the PSC meeting, there is actually not much happening in the meeting that is a great surprise. It's boring. 'Okay, now the Spanish are going to say this and the Germans are going to say that.'"[16] The cycle repeats for the Thursday meeting. This highly regimented, consensus-driven process needs certain kinds of political subjects to participate. While the ambassadors of the member states need not be compliant or obedient, they must be similarly oriented toward consensus.

Technological Infrastructure

One aspect of CFSP that links the various foreign-policy apparatuses of the EU in a relational space are media technologies, which allow both information and affects to circulate through the CFSP assemblage.[17] The earliest technology was the Coreu (Correspondance Européenne) tele-graph network, a set of direct telefax lines that linked the foreign min-istries of the EC, enabling discussion of draft texts to proceed after the ministers had returned to their capitals.

> The ambassadors obviously would go back to their capitals and they would be reporting back and so on. Then say the presidency put 'round a text resulting from a meeting, then you'd see a Coreu telegram from the British saying that we would suggest amending paragraph four, line three, and the French would weigh in and so on. . . . Certainly by the early 1980s people would be talking to each other on the phone quite a lot.[18]

This telegraph network (and later the telephone) was not merely a means to rationally negotiate a collective text; it affected those who were on either end of the telegraph network, reading and writing the telegrams: "Certainly the fact of sharing information creates confidence, if everyday you see Coreus coming in from different countries, and 80 per cent of the Coreus with which you would entirely agree, it is a *constant reaffir-mation* that there is a certain European approach which really does have something in common."[19] Indeed, Coreu became a central connective tissue that facilitated both *European thinking* and *thinking European* with regard to foreign policy. The system, which was created in 1973, tripled over the next twenty years in terms of the number of telegraphs deliv-ered per year, despite the increasing use of the telephone.[20]

While telegrams are no longer the cutting edge of secure com-munications technology, Coreu still serves as the basic template for communication among the EU's foreign ministries, and now with the EEAS. Information security is taken quite seriously, especially given eavesdropping capabilities: "A lot of the documentation is restricted or confidential, so therefore there are all sorts of bits of IT linked to how we can send information to member states."[21] The threat of eavesdrop-ping has undercut the simplicity of the Coreu system in circumstances when highly classified information is to be discussed among EU foreign ministries, because unlike the smooth space of the telegraph network, contemporary secure communications systems tend to be more pro-prietary. Consider, for instance, a recent situation in which a British diplomat wanted to speak with his French, Dutch, and German counter-parts about sanctions on Syria. The discussion required a higher level of information security than is used in everyday diplomacy: secure video teleconferencing (VTC).

> [We only do VTC] in certain circumstances because, believe it or not, amongst friendly nations we don't have the same technology. So when I was chairing these videoconferences with those other three countries, the way we were doing it was that my colleagues went to the local U.K. embassies, sat in our classified video teleconference room and worked . . . using the U.K. network to do it. We don't do that often because it would be a real pain for them, as it would be for me to take a taxi and go to the French embassy.[22]

The striated spaces of information security are a material imposition on the flows of information and affect that compose CFSP. Further efforts at communications interoperability are necessary if this is to change.

A similar situation can be seen in third countries where multiple EU embassies and the EEAS delegation seek to coordinate their activities. For example, in Nairobi the EU embassies began to install a secure communications system in early 2012, but the system required new computers in all the embassies, so it took several years to complete the installation. Prior to this, crucial information was either passed back via secure national telecommunications links to national capitals in order to maintain information security (e.g., from Nairobi to Lisbon, to Paris, and back to Nairobi) or was sent as hard copy via couriers, which was hardly more efficient, as Nairobi's EU embassies can be as much as two hours from each other in traffic.[23]

Recent efforts have been made to increase the interoperability of secure communications within the EU institutions themselves, as this is an even wider problem than the incompatibility of the national communications systems. "The problem was the EU institutions themselves had their own networks. For example, on crisis response and humanitarian relief, the European Commission's ECHO [EU Humanitarian and Civil Protection Department] had its own system, which was incompatible with that of many member states and quite advanced in comparison to that of the European External Action Service, which was built on the existing Coreu system."[24] The problems of interoperability—and the ways in which a lack thereof slows down the reaction speed of CFSP during a crisis—are magnified in the case of the situation room, a networked space of crisis management that has proliferated throughout governments.[25] Each actor (e.g., ECHO, the EEAS, individual member states) has its own situation room, and the real-time communication required to collectively act is hampered by the lack of interoperability.[26] Some of these problems are legacies of past iterations of CFSP. For instance, the EEAS—despite being the newest actor, only a few years old— has a situation room that is inferior to that of ECHO because it is built on the aging material infrastructure of Coreu. Therefore, ongoing refinement of secure communications interoperability via the production of new protocols is currently an agenda item within the CFSP assemblage, and with good reason.

The Embodied Encounter

Topological communications networks are crucial to the day-to-day workings of CFSP, and the regularity of contact they enable reinforces a sense of European commonality. However, I was repeatedly struck in my interviews by the crucial importance of the embodied encounter. "I mean, people send each other e-mails. But because we are so close [in Brussels], there are a lot of meetings, lunches. Yes, a lot of face-to-face meetings and negotiations."[27] I am not alone in this observation; Merje Kuus has written extensively of the specific milieu of the European Quarter.[28] The embodied encounter was crucial to the production of CFSP in two ways. First, it engendered trust among the participants. Second, the political expectations associated with embodied encounter meant that differences of opinion had to be overcome in one way or another in order to produce a result that maintained a positive affective orientation to the collective future.

The topic of trust emerged unprompted in virtually every interview I conducted. Its centrality to CFSP is in direct proportion to the complexity of the CFSP assemblage, through which various capabilities and competencies are distributed (e.g., member states, the European Commission, the EEAS, and so on). "It's very complex, a lot of moving parts and then of course working in very difficult places, which is also part of the complexity. It is amazing that things happen smoothly, because it is a very complex set of actors, and I find trust is very important. Trust between the institutions, trust between individuals."[29] That this interviewee links the first-order bodies politic of individual policy makers and the second-order bodies politic of EU institutions is notable; these affects are transpersonal but also something more than that.

The creation of the EEAS from staff originally working in the European Commission, the Council of Ministers, and the member states has produced some well-documented issues of institutional culture clash.[30] Of note for a discussion of trust is the way in which the creation of the EEAS assemblage has brought together individual diplomats, standardized protocols, and relations with other bodies (whether linked to the European Commission, member states, or third countries).

> In the [European] Commission in the 1990s I think there was a desperate attempt to institutionalize and standardize everything, and essentially take the human element out of policy making. And as long as you do straight policy and development policy, this has worked fairly well. You arrange things, you calculate your numbers and things like that, but when the decision was made to have a diplomatic service and to establish the EEAS, these kind of calculatedly standardized interactions don't function so well.[31]

The proceduralism that the EEAS inherited from the European Commission worked to stifle the affective potentials for trust. If trust was not inherent to the everyday workings of the EEAS, other sites of embodied encounter served to provide the affective grease for the CFSP machinery. Many of these spaces were not explicitly diplomatic spaces, but emerged as such via social encounters in the Brussels milieu or in third-country capitals. "It's a question of socialization, really, in the Brussels bubble, for them to get acquainted with their colleagues, go to each other's receptions and talk on the fringes of meetings or if there are public events, again on the fringes. That socialization part shouldn't be neglected."[32]

Informal sites of diplomacy were not merely places where trust accrued, but also sites in which real policy making occurred, not only in Brussels but in third countries. The research analyst (and political geographer) Veit Bachmann witnessed the work that went into achieving consensus prior to meetings in Nairobi: "I was not able to take part in the political meetings [being not formally attached to a member state delegation], but being still affiliated with the EU delegation, I was invited for dinner parties, and you know, it was really intriguing for me to see, not only talk about things on a working level, but a lot of talk with you and your colleague to sort out if you are going to argue at the morning meeting. And this played a big role."[33] The personal and the professional come to be enmeshed in social situations like this, although the relationships described by my interviewees rarely seemed as long lasting or as meaningful as they did, for instance, in the world of intelligence co-operation.[34] One British respondent described the intimacy among his European counterparts but specifically excluded personal friendship: "They [the French and Germans] are also the people with whom I have the closest personal friendship, and we know each other quite well. *Not in the sense of our personal lives*, but we will form an opinion about each other's ability to . . . stick to deals or suddenly change the deal or do the opposite of what they said. So in a way you build up a picture in your mind about these interlocutors."[35] These relationships might not be long lasting for several reasons, but it is almost certainly due in part to the fact that diplomats tend to rotate in and out of positions within three years, thereby making it less likely to form long-term friendships. This is in contrast to intelligence cooperation, where specialization often funnels individuals down parallel career paths, thereby facilitating friendships.

In addition to trust, the common expectation and desire for a collective future constituted an affective relation crucial to the production of CFSP. This orientation to the future manifests itself in a range of emotional states depending on the circumstances. For instance, in the debate over the original list of sanctions against Russia in response to the Ukraine crisis, this orientation manifested initially as anxiety: "I think the nervousness was less about the fact that it was clear from the discussion that member states were on very different lines, but more the nervousness of 'Are we going to agree on anything?'"[36] This anxiety morphed into relief as the debate unfolded: "After four or five people started to come in and said, 'Look, we think the sanctions should target these people and these people.' It was really obvious to everyone what the compromise is going to be. Even if it was obvious to everyone that they won't get their position, there was this sort of massive sense of relief. Because we all knew, 'God, this is going to be okay. We are going to get a good result here.'"[37] There is more to the collective-future phenomenon than simply wanting to see the CFSP succeed; this common affective orientation is manifested in specific embodied encounters. These embodied encounters are both iterative and performative, and they provide resources with which ambassadors can seek to renegotiate their policy position "back home."

So . . . every ambassador sitting in that room is, if you like, between the will of the room to come to an agreement and the position of their ministry. And sometimes you have a situation where we know going into the meeting that we have a problem with one or two delegations, and those two—by having a first round of discussion and everyone coming out against their position—they will say privately that that's incredibly helpful because they can call their capital and say, "Look, there are twenty-six against this line. Are we really going to be the one to stand out?" *But it has to happen in the room,* you have to perform it because it becomes . . . not public, but it's in front of all the others.[38]

In this way, the embodied encounters of the meeting room help to provide an affective push toward compromise and consensus.

Another type of embodied encounter that contributes to the production of CFSP is the site visit, wherein the foreign ministers (or lower-ranking officials) of all member states visit a location together. The common sensory experience of the landscape at issue can provide a powerful affective marker around which foreign policy can be made, as in the following description: "The point about that trip [to the West Bank] is the fact that everyone saw the situation on the ground. You can't be taken around the settlement areas and see the point where if a block of settlement was built, it would split the Palestinian Authority in two. You actually see that. Then there are certain arguments in these meetings that can't be used because everyone knows this is nonsense; we saw this together."[39] The common physical occupation of space—whether via the meeting room or the site visit—exercises a powerful force for political-subject making among state elites.

Syncing the National, the European, and the Global

Thus far, I have dealt with representatives of the member states as individuals interfacing with the EU's foreign-policy apparatus. Of course, these individuals are also (or even primarily) enmeshed in their states' foreign-policy apparatuses. Their bodies thus serve as conduits for information and affects circulating between the two larger assemblages. There also exist other conduits for information and affects, some of which are not Brussels-based; for instance, each member state has a European correspondent, who is part of a Europe-wide network of contacts in foreign ministries dedicated to communicating about European concerns. This system goes back to the origins of Political Cooperation in the 1970s, and survives despite the elaborate infrastructure of everyday diplomacy introduced in Brussels since then. Hugo Shorter, the European correspondent for the United Kingdom at the time of this research, described his position thus: "I find that I am . . . fairly regularly called upon by different parts of the Foreign Office . . . to resolve negotiation issues that are coming up in the Political and Security Committee or in the Foreign Affairs Council, and I resolve it through discussions and negotiations with this network of European correspondents."[40] The advantage of the European correspondents is precisely that they are *not* in Brussels, but instead are located in their national capitals. When an issue is proving difficult in Brussels, it can be "kicked back" to the national capital, where people with more capacity for flexibility can be found (often, but not always, the ambassadors in Brussels answer to their European correspondent): "Many deals are cooked up in Brussels and representatives in Brussels will check back to see if it is okay. . . . 'Can we do this? Can we do that?' That's fine, but not always, because sometimes people in Brussels are under instructions that don't allow them to make deals. So they have to go back to their capitals and say, 'Can you accept this?' And it's in those situations that I get involved."[41] But what happens when foreign ministries and the institutions of CFSP mangle together? What kind of work must be done to sync the rhythms of these giant apparatuses in order to produce meaningful policy?

Temporalities of Foreign Policy Formation

Charles Tilly noted as early as 1994 that the European project threatened the control over time that had come to be the complete preserve of the nation-state. The rhythms of educational systems, financial transactions, and so on would be (and to some extent have been) brought into some degree of alignment as a result of Europeanization.[42] The same is true of foreign-policy creation. In this section I focus on the ways in which the British Foreign and Commonwealth Office has adapted to the rhythms of CFSP.

Having been in the EU for over forty years at the time of this research, the Foreign and Commonwealth Office (FCO) is well adapted to the rhythms of CFSP. It is not as if they were working away on a completely separate world and every now and then they wake up and say, 'Hey, we're in the EU.' No, the EU is much more part of how the Foreign Office does business across the board."[43] Various FCO departments are constantly engaged with the working groups of the EEAS (whose deliberations filter up to the Political and Security Committee) in areas of their expertise. Larger strategy is produced by inserting FCO preparatory meetings into the CFSP cycle, such that internal agreement can be achieved and agenda items prioritized well in advance. Several weeks before a Foreign Affairs Council meeting, the British strategy is agreed upon in an internal meeting: "What are the angles going to be there, what are the difficult things we need to prepare him [the foreign secretary] for if someone pushes X or Y that we don't like?"[44] Those decisions are then filtered out to the various departments of the FCO.

The way in which these British foreign-policy priorities are produced—not just in the FCO but in all government departments with a European dimension—means that they are more difficult to change in Brussels. Because European issues are circulated in the Cabinet of the United Kingdom to produce policy coherence, every British minister has been briefed and has signed on to the decided policy. "Having decided [policy] like that, it is much more difficult to change it, and because so much goes to the European Council, the incentive for individual ministers to compromise is much less because it's much easier to push it to the prime minister and let him or her take responsibility for selling [it]."[45] Perhaps it is partly for this reason that the United Kingdom has had a reputation in Europe for being a poor partner. In any event, such idiosyncrasies mean that each member state brings its own flexibility (or lack thereof) to the table when it comes to the making of CFSP.

The practices of France and Germany, for example, are in significant contrast to the internal coherence (and rigidity) of British policy making. Since the 1963 Élysée Treaty, France and Germany have hosted semi-annual summits of their leaders, with subsequent anniversaries of the treaty celebrated by the creation of new Franco-German councils at other levels of government.

> One of the clever things that Adenauer and de Gaulle did with the original Franco-German treaty was that they created a structure that obliges people, not just the heads of government but also the cabinet ministers, to meet on a regular basis. And of course no one wants to go to a meeting without results, and when you start looking for results, then you start looking for things where you can get a result. . . . The French and Germans have the sort of relationship where in the last analysis neither will let the other lose out on a very significant national interest.[46]

Whereas British policy is made internally rigid through its process of production, French and German policy is coordinated in the first instance transnationally, which then enables a joint position to emerge among two of the leading states in the EU. Diplomatically, by opening up their policy processes to one another (puissance) France and Germany achieve a stronger bargaining position in Brussels (pouvoir).

Just as the internal idiosyncrasies of member states' foreign-policy apparatuses affect the dynamics of CFSP, the elaborately harmonized dance of foreign-policy formation within the member states and at the scale of CFSP does not occur in a vacuum. Rather, they are situated in and responding to a world of processes unfolding at different temporalities. Therefore, at varying moments the rhythms of CFSP may fail to resonate with the temporalities of the processes into which the EU would like to intervene. Despite all the situation rooms, secure e-mail systems, joint military capabilities, and so on that have emerged within the context of CFSP in recent years, it is clear from the sheer number of meetings (as well as pre-meetings, and pre-pre-meetings) that greasing the wheels of CFSP can be a time-consuming process. "When it concerns crisis issues, which often have to do with war and peace, often the national instinct kicks in, which seems to leave less scope for the coordinating mechanisms that have been created at EU level."[47] As an example, in 2013 France intervened in Mali, to help put down an Islamist rebellion against the interim government, without warning its EU partners, and despite the existence of the Weimar battlegroup, a joint French-Polish-German rapid reaction force formed only two years prior for just such a scenario. "The procedural aspect to early CFSP decision-making was considered to be too lengthy by the French to wait for . . . so they just went for it."[48] There is, of course, also a historical element of colonialism in the French response, which helps to explain the desire to "go it alone." Still, it is apparent that at the timescale of crisis, the EU finds it difficult to reduce response time without impinging on the twin political imperatives of consultation and consensus among the member states.

Other temporal contexts are more conducive to a European response. Key recent examples include both the current situation in Ukraine, in which sanctions are a primary policy lever, and the recently concluded nuclear negotiations with Iran. In both situations the cohesion of CFSP over relatively long periods of time is a key element of European power. However, in these circumstances it is not a question of member states' foreign policy versus CFSP; rather, these are occurring simultaneously. At issue is who is doing what in each particular case. For instance, with regard to the Ukrainian crisis,

> At the highest political level you have [German Chancellor] Angela Merkel calling [Russian President] Putin; it's not [EU High Representative] Ashton calling Putin. . . . But they act in concert nonetheless, these heads of government and heads of state. [French President] Hollande then called, and then [U.S. President] Obama called, and then the G7. It's been a very fluid, at least institutionally fluid period, and it still is. Because they are wearing different hats, they just use the different mechanisms at their disposal.[49]

When Chancellor Merkel calls President Putin, she is simultaneously speaking as the leader of Germany and as a key player in the CFSP. Her embodied performance of diplomacy is feeding into both the complex assemblage of CFSP and also the relatively more decisive (if also complex) German foreign-policy apparatus.

The temporalities of foreign-policy formation are not limited to the crisis or the "ongoing issue." There are also generational dynamics within the staff of the many institutions enrolled in the CFSP. For instance, a range of events and bureaucratic idiosyncrasies have shaped the relationship between the FCO and CFSP from the beginning—or even earlier. Indeed, the long-term perception of the FCO as more pro-Europe than the rest of the British government (or perhaps the British people) originated during the traumatic pre-accession years: "There was a generation of people [in the FCO] who were perhaps not the generation involved in the decision not to join in 1957, but who were scarred by the fact that we didn't join. . . . They were determined that that mistake shouldn't be made again, and then of course being vetoed twice by de Gaulle was very humiliating."[50] This trauma produced within the body politic of the FCO a collective memory that lasted well into the contemporary period. It manifested materially as the FCO's economy of prestige: to be assigned to one of the two European departments within the FCO was a mark of distinction, a sign that you were going places. This distinction created a virtuous circle, wherein talented people would prioritize European specialization, which in turn would produce European issues as a priority.

However, several factors have recently undermined this virtuous circle. The first is the diffusion of knowledge about the EU throughout government. While the FCO remains the go-to department for European issues, the departments responsible for agriculture, justice, trade, taxes, and other issues have gained in-house expertise and increasingly engage with the EU on their own. Therefore, the FCO monopoly on Europe has been undermined horizontally, as the web of foreign relations increasingly bypasses the European department. The second factor is the rise of the prime minister's office in European affairs (and in other foreign affairs besides). "Though the foreign secretary formally remains the coordinator of business, in practice much more is done head of government to head of government, and offices of prime ministers communicate directly with their opposite numbers."[51] The FCO monopoly on Europe has thus also been undermined vertically, as the prime minister participates more actively in European affairs. With Europe therefore holding less of a prestige position within the FCO, the foreign-policy apparatus appears to be "forgetting" the trauma of the early years and aligning more closely with the rest of the government in its attitudes to the EU and by extension to CFSP. Though it is not always apparent in the CFSP's day-to-day workings, CFSP dynamics occur over the *longue durée*.

Rethinking the National Interest

Having sought to demonstrate the complex ways in which power, affects, and policy emerge from the bodies politic enrolled in the production of the CFSP, I now consider the ways in which the processes of the CFSP have reworked the "national interest" of its member states. Traditionally, the CFSP is understood as the product of these national interests, mediated by the EU institutions. By inverting the equation, I emphasize the mutual becoming of foreign-policy apparatuses in the national capitals and Brussels.

The CFSP has been acting back on the member states that collectively compose it in part through a "practice of initiative," which has been increasingly exercised by the EU high representative since the Lisbon Treaty entered into force. Given that the EU controls access, in many cases, to more intelligence on a specific issue than any individual member (excepting perhaps the United Kingdom), and because the EEAS now chairs meetings both of the Foreign Affairs Council and in third countries, the EU is able to shape the agenda and the terms of debate on many issues for most member states. This is, to be fair, largely due to the apathy of many member states on many issues; where member states have strong interests (or their own sources of intelligence), they are less susceptible to this subtle form of power. But only a few member states have global foreign-policy interests and strong capabilities in intelligence and related fields.

A recent example demonstrates the subtle power of CFSP over member state political cognition. Serbia's desire to join the EU has given the EEAS leverage in pushing for a conclusion to the contested status of Kosovo. First, EEAS counselor Robert Cooper and then the then EU high representative, Catherine Ashton, facilitated a series of roughly twenty meetings between the prime ministers of Serbia and Kosovo in hopes of normalizing their relations. The subsequent agreement received the unanimous backing of the Foreign Affairs Council, which is notable given that five member states do not recognize Kosovo. "The accession talks with Serbia are preparing the ground ultimately for the recognition by Serbia of Kosovo's independence to secure its integration into the EU, which will pave the way for those five outlier member states who have not recognized Kosovo for reasons that have to do with their own national interests to change their position."[52] Therefore, the EEAS—through its occupation of a policy space that gives some room for initiative independent of the member states—is able to shape agendas in ways that make the member states rethink their own interests.

Another way in which CFSP influences the foreign policies of its member states is simply by its role as a "multiplier of what we want to achieve."[53] In short, participating in CFSP enables policy makers to expand their horizons with regard to what their interests might be, what they might be able to achieve, and who "they" are. Countries that might not otherwise take a position on the Russian invasion of Crimea or on Iranian nuclear policy now feel they should. Simultaneously, individual policy makers (and their broader foreign-policy apparatuses) are emboldened by the solidarity that can come with CFSP. This has explicit foreign-policy impacts. In the 1970s, for example, British support for Palestine in the 1970s was contrary to American foreign policy, and Henry Kissinger accused the British at the time of ruining the Special Relationship, a charge that is normally the third rail of British foreign policy; however, in this case Sir Alex Douglas-Home took a stand, noting that this was not just a British policy but a *European* one. "The safety of numbers is quite a big fact."[54]

As one FCO official put it, the effect of CFSP on British foreign policy is two-fold: "Being in the EU does change our own foreign policy objectives to the extent that (a) our perceptions are broadened by our intimate dialogue with others with different perceptions, and (b) we might do trades with them on particular issues where we can advance an interest there when we see something that is less important to us."[55] Of particular interest is the embodied nature of the FCO official's first point, in which it is the change in sensibilities produced through a relation of "intimacy" that brings about a different subjectivity, with different interests. In short, the self is reframed in a broader way. This is also evident in the official's more Realpolitik-inflected second point, in which bargains are struck. Even this, though, illustrates an understanding of diplomacy that is far from a zero-sum game, positing instead that "we" can all get something we want if others' needs are internalized as just as worthy as our own and therefore in need of accommodation. This is not a purely rational decision, but rather a mode of decision-making that is habituated and materialized through the iterative and bureaucratic nature of decision-making within CFSP.

Given the various temporalities at which processes unfold within the various foreign-policy apparatuses that compose the CFSP assemblage, it is still too soon to know all the ways in which CFSP—in its latest material form—will shape the foreign policies of the member states. But indicators are available where there have been changes in funding, new states, or other contextual shifts that provide opportunities for dynamism. The recent financial crisis, for example, sparked a round of retrenchment in many European diplomatic services. "A lot of member states [cut] their diplomatic networks, closing embassies, consulates abroad, and even pushing for the EU to take on some consular tasks for which it is not equipped nor has the competence to do that type of thing."[56] Reliance on the EEAS is uneven, as member states such as France, Germany, and the United Kingdom have maintained (or even grown) their global diplomatic footprint. Nevertheless, as many smaller member states have closed embassies, or co-located their embassies with other EU states or the EEAS delegation, the physical context has made close coordination within the CFSP more likely with regard to these third countries.

Perhaps indicative of these trends is the EU compound in Juba, South Sudan. Capital of the newest recognized state in the world, Juba offers a glimpse into a potential future for EU diplomacy in that its diplomatic quarter is entirely new, reflecting current visions of CFSP and its relational spaces. Here, I am reliant on the insights of the political geographer Veit Bachmann, who visited in 2012. He noted that six of the eight EU member states with embassies in Juba had located their facilities within the walled EU compound (which also hosts the EU delegation). "In Juba, it is the EU compound in which the daily (professional) lives of European diplomats are concentrated. Diplomats from the member states and the delegation are located in the same place; through physical proximity, they interact on a daily basis—not only professionally but also privately as part of a joint interest in having a social life."[57] The newness of Juba as a world capital has offered an "experimental laboratory" for CFSP, both with regard to the production of a cohesive collective foreign policy (pouvoir), but also with regard to the cohesive collective (puissance). Bachmann notes,

> Asking people for the embassies of individual EU member states usually is a fruitless endeavor, whereas the location of the EU compound is widely known. In some ways, the EU compound, as a physical place of European collectivity, has achieved what the EU as a geopolitical actor seeks to attain—it is recognized as an entity. Interestingly, the supposedly remote location of Juba might be one of the first where the EU's ambition to develop *collective* geopolitical agency materializes.[58]

While in no way indicative of *the* future, Juba is the materialization of *a* future for CFSP, one in which it is increasingly impossible to disentangle the member states' policies from that of the EU, or to know whose interests are emerging triumphant through the foreign-policy assemblage. It is notable that this is occurring in a country that is (for the Europeans anyway) something of a tabula rasa, and in which individual member states have few strong national interests.

Because Juba is so idiosyncratic, it cannot be considered a teleological waypoint through which CFSP must pass on its way to an idealized future. Rather, it is one specific instantiation of a complex foreign-policy assemblage that in some times and places will be marked by strong coherence and a relatively hierarchical organization through which pouvoir is generated (as in Juba), and in other times and places will remain the self-organizing, improvisational enterprise that has marked most of CFSP's history. Just as there are those who seek to advance CFSP as part of a progressive understanding of the European project, there are those who will seek to undermine it in order to protect national prerogatives. More accurately, the same people will advocate for coherent action in some circumstances and will question the EU's competency in foreign affairs in other circumstances. Indeed, rather than offering an institutionalist appreciation of CFSP that seeks to define what it is and what it does, I have demonstrated the need for scholars to appreciate the powerful forces unleashed *within* CFSP that shape both the policies emerging from the EU and the policy makers who work within it.

Studying Geopolitical Assemblages

I have sketched out a vision of international relations foregrounding the actual relations that compose the international. Where others have looked to macroscaled geographic entities such as civilizations or even the "international community" (a stand-in for civilization itself) to explain patterns in the behavior of states, I have instead looked to the microscaled bodies, things, and practices that collectively affect foreign-policy making in the grand sense. My selection of case studies has emphasized the fact that in various fields of British foreign policy (diplomacy, intelligence, defense), the state apparatus intended to act in the world is already enmeshed in that world and affected by it. This enmeshing may be institutionalized in the form of international organizations (NATO, the EU), or it may be a set of cooperative practices shared with other states (traditional diplomacy, intelligence cooperation).

Each of these particular fields is unique in its development and points to a different "civilizational" identity: for UKUSA, the Anglosphere; for NATO, the West; and for the CFSP, Europe. While each field to a certain extent helps constitute the macroscaled geographic entity to which it corresponds, it is more fruitful to consider the way in which these fields intersect in the foreign-policy apparatuses of the states composing them. The simultaneity of these assemblages' becoming hints at the ways in which they cannot be so easily separated into case studies or chapters of a book; they can also be understood as a single assemblage with certain "hub" states such as the United Kingdom serving as an affective conduit between them. The top-secret development of UKUSA hindered the development of intelligence cooperation in NATO, with intelligence hived off from the competency of MAS. Similarly, the existence (and American-led capabilities) of NATO have haunted the creation of CFSP, with the French historically trying to prioritize CFSP over NATO and the Germans and British advocating national competency in foreign policy to help keep the United States committed to European defense. The simultaneity of all these processes pushes us to conceptualize them not as bounded territories (the West, the Anglosphere, etc.) but as a web of material circulations: digital information, standardized jet fuel, bureaucrats going to conferences, Coreu messages, STANAGs, and so on. These material circulations are of various intensities, composing a relational space that is qualitatively uneven and always in flux.

Some might claim that centering on the United Kingdom skews this study, as it is a thoroughly enmeshed state, while most states are not. There is some truth to this; Britain is at the heart of many geopolitical assemblages, a material legacy of its past role as a global hegemon. However, all states are to some degree enmeshed in the outside world. As I demonstrated in chapter 1, even basic diplomacy entails some degree of *puissance*, and basic diplomacy (of some sort) is one of the performances crucial to the generation of state effects. In any event, these case studies are indicative of the potential in this theoretical approach, rather than representative of either all states or all types of geopolitical assemblage.

It would also be easy to narrate the case studies in this volume as a response to conditions of globalization. For instance, the first case study—of the nineteenth-century British Foreign Office—is clearly indebted to time-space compression and other concepts associated with globalization.[1] In chapters 2 and 3 I tell, in slightly different ways, tales of the Anglo-American-led globalization of different kinds of governmental practices (intelligence cooperation and interoperability). But to collapse these narratives into exemplars of globalization is to miss out on key insights that can be drawn from them, largely because of the often teleological nature of much globalization discourse.

What emerges from these stories is the highly contingent nature of these assemblages' territorialization and coding. Perhaps the most apparent of these is UKUSA intelligence cooperation, which is essentially a freak historical accident that has not been replicated anywhere else to the degree that it has been within UKUSA. Quite frankly, intelligence cooperation during peacetime such as we see in UKUSA is not supposed to happen, let alone last for seventy years. It is not difficult to imagine a world in which wartime collaboration came to an end on VJ Day. Indeed, all kinds of paradoxical lines of flight might have led to such an outcome. Recall that one of the drivers for collaboration on both sides of the Atlantic was the fear of looming budget cuts. If the U.S. and U.K. governments, recognizing the importance of signals intelligence in the coming Cold War, had maintained or only slightly cut their budgets, UKUSA might not have happened. There were certainly voices in the U.S. armed forces that were opposed to the collaboration.

As the most recent development, the CFSP of the EU is perhaps the easiest case study to see as contingent; in fact, pundits constantly debate the future of CFSP.[2] Will it remain fragmented and incoherent, or will it transform the EU into a major player on the world stage? But now is not the only moment when the future of CFSP has seemed unclear. Rather, the number of moments in which Political Cooperation might have remained the limit of harmonization—or even collapsed—boggles the mind. In chapters 3 and 4 (on NATO and CFSP, respectively), I included particular affect-saturated orientations to the future as forces within the machinery of everyday diplomacy that drove forward the project, as with Dwight Eisenhower's concern that a lack of progress on interoperability would call into question the whole future of collective security that NATO was pioneering. Similarly, when EU ambassadors sit down in the Political and Security Committee for a contentious vote (as with regard to sanctions on Russia), anxiety over the possibility of failed consensus overrides most countries' desire to get their own way and enables agreements to be made. While both of these cases involve positive scenarios, the inverse scenario would involve a lack of progress, for whatever reason—in interoperability or in EU foreign-policy making—that could cause the affective forces generating coherence (optimism, solidarity) to give way to deterritorializing affects, such as disappointment and fear. I have studied successful (thus far) assemblages in that *they exist*; it remains for future researchers to look at completely deterritorialized geopolitical assemblages of the past (and virtual assemblages that were never actualized).

In parallel to the lack of teleological growth of these assemblages, the impact of the assemblages on states' foreign-policy formation is far from determinative. The 2003 invasion of Iraq and the (nonexistent) 2013 intervention in Syria by the United States and United Kingdom make that clear. The "inclining logic" of the Anglo-American special relationship does not mean that—despite many pundits' claims— Britain is swept along in America's wake and must follow suit.[3] Nor does it mean that these countries are more likely to go to war than to not. Nevertheless, as Srdjan Vucetic notes, there is an empirically measurable effect of these assemblages in that they tend to "flock together."[4] The unexpected deflation of the 2013 Syria crisis is just as much an example of the inclining logic of geopolitical assemblages as is the 2003 Iraq invasion. Parliament's surprise vote against intervention rippled through American policy as well. In this particular case, the inclining logic of assemblage led to peace (of a sort) where it might have been otherwise.[5]

What are we left with if we reject the teleology of globalization and a shallow set of policy implications based on determinism? What remains is a more-than-human political ontology that rejects stasis and structure in favor of dynamism and becoming, and that locates power in the unfolding of processes in a range of relational spaces and over vastly different timescales. The nonhuman dimension of geopolitical assemblages obliges us to think in new spatial and temporal registers that are uncomfortable, or nearly beyond our ability to sense. Some of these spaces might be very small, such as the locked file cabinets protecting the secret of CREAM after World War II, or they may be conventional (if new and unique) diplomatic spaces such as the EU compound in Juba, South Sudan. They may be virtually global, such as the network of EU delegations around the world or the UKUSA eavesdropping apparatus. Likewise, the temporalities of these systems' unfolding are a multiplicity, from the glimmer of affect in a side-room diplomatic encounter to the generational impact of events on the staff of a foreign ministry (such as de Gaulle's veto of U.K. membership in the EC, or the 2016 Brexit vote for the United Kingdom to withdraw from the EU). Longer still are some of the cycles of war materiel production; the United States continues to fly B-52 planes first designed immediately after World War II. Perhaps longer still is the investment in a building for the foreign ministry; the FCO continues to work with, renovate, and improvise using the space designed by George Gilbert Scott 150 years ago. Considering the ways in which these spaces and temporalities intersect and resonate (or not) offers a problematic through which we might approach this new ontology.

And what is the role of the human in all these processes? Described in this way, geopolitical assemblages sound every bit as teleological and disempowering as globalization discourse: vast processes unfolding in geologic time. However, as reflective and intentional elements of geopolitical assemblages, humans remain central to any analysis. What differs here from most other approaches to international relations or geopolitics is the conceptualization of the political subject. A political subject is the emergent outcome of processes of assemblage—a first-order body politic, to use John Protevi's term.[6] Therefore, processes of political cognition and action are inexorably shaped by the context in which they are unfolding, as was apparent to the nineteenth-century select committees that debated the future Foreign Office and the kinds of affective atmospheres that might be inculcated within it.

That example, though, also shows the importance of human reflexivity to these processes of assemblage; it is only the human elements of an assemblage that can be self-aware of these processes and act on them as a project of the self. This was true not only in the nineteenth century; it was evident through the microengineering of spaces in all the twentieth- and twenty-first-century case studies as well. For instance, the creators of UKUSA attempted to engineer atmospheres of trust into the famously secretive spaces of national security by allowing senior liaisons freedom of movement in each other's intelligence agencies, and also in the frequent use of secondments. Similarly, a European political subject was seen to arise out of the workings of CFSP, such as the constant arrival of Coreu messages and the iterative nature of meetings through which consensus was achieved (or a topic abandoned). While the nonhuman must be understood through its capacities for self-organization and affect, it must also be understood as a set of resources, inherited from the past, with which human agents can improvise, adapt, and enact *pouvoir*. Like the bricks pried from the street by Dickens's mob, they contribute to the affective atmosphere and the capabilities of the assemblage but not always in the ways we expect. The human capacity to shape and control assemblages will always be marked by an excess, or slippage, in which vital materials exert themselves to produce nonlinear outcomes.[7]

Reassembling the Case Studies

Having recapitulated my theoretical claims with reference to the specific case studies in this book, I now turn to some key findings of the research. Read from start to finish, this book offers a counterhistory of British foreign-policy making, which instead of emphasizing the role of Britain in the world traces the ways in which the world is increasingly inside British foreign-policy making. This emphasis on the subject-making power of affect and sociomaterial assemblages complicates the accounts of diplomacy and statecraft that have emerged in the Practice Turn. While this excellent work has quite rightly shifted attention to the "virtuosity" of diplomats and other embodied actors, it has rarely attributed much agency to the technologies, materials, and sites in which diplomacy unfolds. A more distributed form of agency highlights the prepersonal politics that unfolds in a range of temporalities and spaces that strict attention to human practices will miss. Those micropractices must be held in view alongside the macroshifts in technologies, institutions, and systems in order to trace the force relations that compose the diplomatic self in any given place or time.

While this volume can be read as a counterhistory, as both histories of specific geopolitical assemblages and also thick descriptions of their everyday diplomacies, the case studies can also be read transversally. I now do so by tracing four themes that cut across all the case studies and offer directions for further research.

Protocol and Puissance

All four case studies dealt, in one way or another, with protocol. I have taken up the term largely from its diplomatic context, where it refers to a slowly evolving set of practices through which states recognize one another. As President Bill Clinton described it, "Protocol evolves in step with our transition to interdependence. By upholding traditions, acknowledging customs, and maintaining appropriate formalities in our interactions with other nations, we convey respect and order, helping to create an environment conducive to mutual understanding and collaborative decision-making."[8] As described here, protocols are formal performances of historical legacies that enable international relations. More interesting, however, is Clinton's description of the *effect* of protocol: order, mutual understanding, and collaborative decision-making. In short, protocol stabilizes the interactions of foreign-policy apparatuses and enables each to affect the other, what Latour referred to as puissance. Of course, the content of diplomacy is a different matter, and can have all kinds of affects. But stripped down to its basics, diplomatic protocol is about interdependence and mutuality.

Another field from which I borrow the term *protocol* is computer networking. In this field a protocol is "a set of rules, algorithms, messages, and other mechanisms that enables software and hardware in networked devices to communicate effectively."[9] For two computers linked in a network, it is the protocol—installed and operating on both sides—that enables communication. This definition is parallel to the usage of *protocol* in diplomacy, but where diplomatic protocol is largely an embodied practice, network protocols are *things*: digital code perpetually humming along in the background of our networked lives.[10] The beauty of network protocols is that they are invisible when functioning correctly.

Both forms of protocol—embodied performance and material object—are useful when considering the everyday diplomacies of assemblage. Analysis of protocols must go beyond simply noting that they enable puissance, however crucial that is. Rather, it is the coding and form of specific protocols that enable particular capacities to emerge. This has been clear in the case studies I have presented in this volume.

In the nineteenth-century Foreign Office, the relevant protocol was traditional diplomatic protocol, as described by President Clinton. The specific coding of diplomatic protocol in the case of the Foreign Office came to matter. In the select-committee meetings for the new Foreign Office, there was a debate over whether or not the new building should include a state dining room in which the foreign secretary could host dinners for the London diplomatic corps. As a materialized site of encounter for the representatives of sovereigns, laden with the formal repertoire of diplomatic performance, this dining room can be understood as a protocol of sorts; it would structure the way in which puissance unfolded in situ. Particularly noteworthy, however, is that the diplomatic corps had theretofore been small enough that the foreign secretary was expected to host these dinners *in his own home*—implying, of course, that only an aristocrat with suitable personal wealth could serve as foreign secretary. Therefore, the dining room was not just a dining room; as a protocol it both enabled diplomacy to occur but also coded the resulting assemblage in particular (aristocratic) ways. The eventual Locarno

Suite, attached to the Foreign Office, offered a different affective atmosphere for the endeavor.

In UKUSA intelligence cooperation, there are many protocols from which to choose. One such protocol was the rotary flywheel of the Combined Cypher Machine (CCM), which materialized the wartime alliance by providing the crucial encryption-decryption link between the two SIGINT networks, enabling them to communicate with one another (see fig. 2.1). The flywheel unleashed the forces of puissance that subtly reworked over many years the intelligence services of the United States, the United Kingdom, Australia, New Zealand, and Canada. Again, however, it did not do *just* this; it was engineered both to enable the flow of information within the wartime alliance and also to prevent that information from falling into enemy hands. Indeed, the relative success of the Allies in cracking Axis codes (and in maintaining that secret) was decisive in the outcome of the war. Therefore, the CCM rotary flywheel could not be replaced with just any other protocol that enabled communication; its material form was coded in particular ways that were essential to the long-term success of the UKUSA assemblage.

The NATO interoperability case study emphasizes both aspects of protocol, the embodied and the material. These protocols enable NATO both to act together and to affect one another. The coding of these protocols matters immensely. The selection of the NATO standard round had implications for how soldiers would be trained, and therefore for the development of NATO tactics and doctrine. It is possible to go one step further, and connect this case study with the existing literature on interoperability, which tends to focus on the political economy of weapons production.[11] Interoperability is often assumed to be a vehicle for the dominance of a few countries within the arms market, and while this is a limited view of the phenomenon—it speaks not at all to procedural interoperability, for instance—there is undoubtedly some truth in the claim that foreign-policy apparatuses seek to steer munitions contracts to their own national companies. Recall, for instance, the Daniel Report of 1979 and its narrowly economistic view of the "two-way street" in European and American weapons production. Therefore, the specific coding of technical protocols in the field of war materiel certainly has implications well beyond the ability of NATO militaries to link up and fight together.

The protocols that enable the CSFP to function are highly bureaucratic and procedural, although a range of material infrastructures, such as the

Coreu network, have aided its development. Face-to-face meetings also function as a form of protocol, both in informal spaces (such as dinner parties) and also in various pre-meetings (prior to the semi-weekly Political and Security Committee meetings or the monthly Foreign Affairs Council meeting). These more informal meetings are notable in that they are a form of *anti*protocol; by operating more casually it becomes possible to work out a consensus-based approach in which there are few surprises in the "official" meeting. While this is an ad hoc, informal system rather than a rigid protocol, it is precisely its flexibility and versatility that codes the resulting assemblage and enables CFSP to emerge at all.

Protocol, in this study, emerges as a crucial concept across all the case studies. It can take many different forms in a range of different assemblages, but, importantly, it is not a *neutral* concept, which merely enables assemblages to enmesh with one another. The actual properties—and thus the capacities—of the protocol come to matter in quite specific ways that must be analyzed in each case.

Hierarchy and Pouvoir

If protocol and puissance are central to the emergence and affects of geopolitical assemblages, it is equally important to remember that in each case study in this volume there is a degree of human intentionality behind the production of these assemblages. While to a certain extent there is an awareness by the institutional architects of the power of puissance, more often than not their stated intent is to enhance the state's pouvoir: the new Foreign Office building was to enhance the United Kingdom's ability to influence other states; UKUSA intelligence cooperation was to achieve near-global surveillance; NATO interoperability was to achieve a transnational fighting force that could defend Western Europe; and CFSP was to give the countries of the EC (now the EU) political clout to match their economic clout. In each case, foreign-policy apparatuses enter into larger assemblages in hopes of achieving greater capability than they would otherwise have.

However, being able to enter into assemblage and being able to control that assemblage are quite different things. Given the diffuse nature of agency within an assemblage, the evolution of an assemblage is not easily shaped, nor is the resulting pouvoir necessarily directed in the vector desired by policy makers embedded within a state apparatus. One of the particularly generative insights of complexity theory is that assemblages, marked by heterogeneity and disorder, can produce order *on their own*, through processes of self-organization. It is for this reason that functionalist accounts of institutions fail to grasp the sheer variety of affective forces at work within these bureaucracies. There is no need for a human hand on the tiller, and indeed that human hand may be insufficient to control the processes at work within the assemblage. As with markets, it is often (but certainly not always) desirable to leave processes of self-organization to themselves, rather than interfere with them. As one FCO employee told me regarding the diplomatic potential of social media (another technocultural assemblage into which foreign-policy apparatuses have become enmeshed), "You can see how much power is in social networks, but when you try to use them, it slips away between your fingers."[12] Such is the hazard of pouvoir in geopolitical assemblages; it is generated by forces largely outside of your control, and therefore is not necessarily susceptible to cooptation. Maintaining the balance between the fluidity of self-organization and the imposition of hierarchy—allowing the assemblage to generate pouvoir and also utilizing that power without ruining it—is a challenge that can often be perceived only over long periods of time.

Two of the geopolitical assemblages I have described are explicitly bureaucratic and institutional, thereby indicating an attempt to impose hierarchy on the processes from the beginning. As a government department, the nineteenth-century Foreign Office might have been expected to work through hierarchies. Indeed, there was an explicit attempt to organize space within the new building in ways that were generative of pouvoir for the foreign secretary and the permanent undersecretary, while undercutting the power of puissance. Edmund Hammond's idealized layout for the new building located senior clerks near him, with junior clerks located beyond the senior clerks. Further, Hammond's efforts to firmly territorialize the Foreign Office by excluding non-Foreign Office workers from the building and maintaining a private library and archive on-site worked to exclude outside influences. This historical moment can be laid alongside other traditional foreign-ministry attempts to govern the effects of puissance on the subjectivities of their employees. For instance, while diplomats overseas are meant to enmesh themselves in their host societies, thereby gaining entry to the halls of power and garnering valuable intelligence and influence, the affective hazard of such a mission must be counteracted by practices such as rotating diplomats on relatively tight timeframes so that they do not "go native."

NATO has similarly struggled to strike the right balance between hierarchy and self-organization. Here, the bottom-up processes through which interoperability is negotiated (based on field experience) are both an asset and also a liability. First, the cost of producing interoperability means that governments want to impose priorities with regard to which capabilities are produced and which are left to the side. Second, the lack of planning from above has occasionally led to discordant efforts to achieve interoperability, as, for instance, between the land and sea boards. A number of institutional efforts have sought to impose order on the processes of self-organization at work, such as the appointment of the first director of MAS in 1955 and the AC/308 review in 1980. These attempts to shape the production of interoperability have nevertheless maintained a relatively hands-off approach, and today only 5 percent of new standards are produced through top-down processes.

The other two case studies are of non-institutional assemblages, in that there is no overarching authority to impose hierarchy. CFSP most closely resembles the institutional model, in that it has a secretariat in the EEAS (though this is relatively new). However, CFSP emerges from the interaction not only of the member states but also of the EEAS and the European Commission (and to a limited extent the European Parliament). The story of Political Cooperation and the eventual turn to CFSP is one of two-steps-forward, one-step-back integration, with the complexity of the arrangements being a direct reflection of the desire of (some) member states to protect their national competency in foreign affairs while also maximizing the collective political power of the European Union. The creation of the EEAS was itself a controversial move intended to provide leadership and coherence to CFSP (thereby maximizing pouvoir) without undermining the member states. The long-term ability of the member states to hold off the puissance of CFSP is as yet unknown.

UKUSA intelligence cooperation is, like the world of traditional diplomacy, a decentered world in which there is no central secretariat or authority. Indeed, UKUSA emerged from completely bottom-up processes of collaboration occurring on the battlefields of Europe and the Pacific. Today, much of the bottom-up cooperation between participating countries occurs in the realms of technology, mathematics, and computing. Due to the specialized knowledge in play, this work often escapes the control of the higher-ups; one retired U.K. intelligence official referred to "cryptographers holding conferences about elliptic curves or other mysterious things which I never understood."[13] This does not mean that power is exclusively bottom-up in UKUSA. These are, after all, quasi-military organizations.

The SIGINT agencies of the "five-eyes" countries are so thoroughly enmeshed as to be inseparable. Technologies, people, and information circulate *within* the bureaucracy in a way that seems to fundamentally remake the national SIGINT agencies into something singular and transnational. The asymmetry among the SIGINT agencies' capabilities means that in practice U.S. (and to a lesser extent the U.K.) policy makers are able to direct the assemblage. For instance, when New Zealand declared its territorial waters nuclear-free, in 1987, it was locked out of UKUSA meetings by the United States although there was no institutional mechanism through which such action might be taken. This unilateral policy remained in place until after the 9/11 attacks, when the United States decided to lift the intelligence embargo.[14] As with NATO (where on paper the United States is just another treaty signatory), hierarchy emerges within an assemblage through a wide array of informal practices. Processes of self-organization are thus a crucial source of the generative power of geopolitical assemblages, but efforts to direct this emergent power can undermine the very source of power meant to be coopted. Empirical investigation is necessary to understand the particularities of power within a given assemblage, identifying spaces and times in which intervention can lead to the successful redirection of the assemblage's emergent agency.

Negotiating Difference

Another key theme from the case studies is the relationship between a given geopolitical assemblage and difference. While to some extent the geopolitical assemblages studied in this volume are defined by the harmonization of practices, affects, and political cognition (via protocols) across the foreign-policy apparatuses that compose them, this does not mean that all difference is evacuated and that foreign-policy apparatuses collapse into one another. In each circumstance a unique multiplicity of difference is accommodated within an assemblage. To claim this is not to impute some intrinsic nature to the assemblage itself, but to recognize that there are a near infinite number of possible arrangements of the assemblage in relational space, and that past certain thresholds these arrangements indicate a collapse of the current assemblage and the possibility of something new.[15] The actual forms of these assemblages do not speak to such virtual possibilities, but they do speak to the variety of ways in which difference can be accommodated.

A spectrum of relations to difference can be found across the case studies. Perhaps least tolerant of difference is UKUSA intelligence cooperation, which might best be understood not as cooperation at all, but as a single bureaucracy to which all five participating countries contribute resources (financial, technical, and human). The standardization of language translations, of technology, and even of the formatting of reports is nearly total. As one of my interviewees stated, the alliance is so successful in part because it is impossible for policy makers to determine the country of origin for any particular intelligence report. The aim is to homogenize as much as possible the participating intelligence apparatuses, a phenomenon best witnessed through the institutional morphology of the participating SIGINT (and counterintelligence) agencies in the wake of the UKUSA alliance.

At the other end of the spectrum is NATO interoperability, in which all member states are required to participate, but which accommodates a huge amount of difference. Participation in any specific NATO mission requires full interoperability on all military capabilities that are mission-specific. While this could be understood as pressing for UKUSA-style total harmonization, the specific texts of STANAGs allow three possible outcomes for processes of standardization: compatibility, interchangeability, and commonality. Commonality refers to UKUSA-style harmonization, while interchangeability refers to the production of multiple avenues through which equipment can be used together, such as the use of adaptors to connect otherwise unharmonized equipment. Compatibility refers to a lack of negative interactions when equipment is used near or with other equipment. This specific framework—in which national differences are allowed to persist—is augmented by the often lax deadlines for agreed-on standards to be implemented (a decade is not uncommon). In recognition of the fact that complete commonality in war materiel is highly unlikely given the range of economic and other interests involved, NATO has long embraced a flexible approach to interoperability in which clusters of countries who are able to work together are encouraged to do so, even if not all NATO countries can follow suit. Difference is understood as an acceptable price for progress in interoperability, wherever it can be had.

Between these two extremes are the case studies of diplomacy: both the traditional diplomacy of the nineteenth century and the more bureaucratized European diplomacy through which CFSP emerges. As Iver Neumann notes, foreign ministries have increasingly come to resemble each other in terms of their organization because it is useful in terms of knowing whom to address in another government's foreign ministry or embassy.[16] The tendency toward harmonization is, of course, uneven and historically contingent. Idiosyncracies abound in the world of traditional diplomacy, such as the confusing naming of the American foreign ministry ("Department of State") or the convoluted history of high commissions within the Commonwealth of Nations.[17] This is in part because of the importance of diplomatic heritage as a material resource, from which states draw legitimacy through their contemporary diplomatic performances.

The production of CFSP is marked by many such idiosyncrasies; each member state has its own policy-making processes, which result from the evolution of the foreign-policy apparatus in that particular state. The particular techniques of the British government made for a strong and coherent policy prior to engagement in Brussels, and subsequently made it difficult to concede ground in negotiation there (for good or ill). Similarly, the role of the European correspondent is common to all member states, but has a distinct institutional position. In some countries the ambassador to the EU answers to the European correspondent in the national capital, and in other countries she or he does not. Therefore, successfully negotiating this political landscape and knowing which levers to pull to achieve your aims requires a great deal of idiosyncratic knowledge that can be gained only through time in Brussels. Ultimately, political concerns over competency in foreign affairs means that there is little enthusiasm for standardization of foreign-affairs apparatuses within the EU.

Therefore, it is impossible to assume that processes of assemblage lead inexorably to the eradication of national difference, as is often assumed in the cruder versions of the globalization literature. Rather, because these are largely bottom-up processes, we can see the formation of order from complexity, with excess that cannot be exterminated. It is important to keep these gaps between homogeneity and heterogeneity within view, as they are the source of potential mutations and interactions that can upend the status quo. These particular quirks and historical holdovers remain potent resources for entrepreneurial subjects who seek to shape the assemblage's becoming in particular ways. It is with that particular agenda in mind—that of active intervention in the face of the seemingly overweening emergent political and military agencies of these geopolitical assemblages—that I turn to the final crosscutting theme of this volume.

Vulnerabilities and Capabilities

A recent critique of relational and materialist work claims that it is insufficiently critical: that by tracing the emergence of an assemblage, the assemblage is reified and alternative arrangements are left unconsidered. This volume has spoken to this critique through a methodological approach; through thick description of these geopolitical assemblages' evolution and everyday practices, I have explicitly sought to identify lines of flight that might have made the world otherwise. Moreover, a critical commitment to praxis and a more progressive world must be rooted in an understanding of political change that comprehends the potentials and vulnerabilities of existing assemblages, rather than a naïve understanding of change that might misdirect scarce political energies.

Nevertheless, there is a danger of highlighting these transnational webs of relations and—despite the explicit aims of assemblage theory to locate power throughout a range of sites—to sketch a world in which powerful state apparatuses not only dominate their territories, but collaborate in order to increase their power. However, this danger is somewhat mitigated by the turn to materiality, which reminds us that the transnational governmentality in which these state apparatuses are enmeshed is predicated on specific materialities, located in specific sites. The materialities enabling the capabilities these state apparatuses seek to deploy are simultaneously vulnerabilities.

This dynamic is most evident in the case study of the nineteenth-century Foreign Office, in which the affective forces unleashed by a changing diplomatic system activated the material vulnerabilities of the Downing Street building. The archive itself—a materiality central to the capability of the Foreign Office to shape world events—proved to be a hindrance to the efficient deployment of state power over many years (for instance, the library shelves were three-deep and distributed virtually without system through the Office). A similar situation was evident in the UKUSA case study, in which the capability of the alliance to sweep almost all global communications into its servers was revealed as limited by the alliance's analytic and storage capacity. Despite technological innovation, there simply is no way to comprehensively examine all the SIGINT that comes through the door. The NSA built a data storage center in Utah in 2013 specifically to store data longer for analysis before deleting it to make room for the constant flood of incoming data, but—like the Whitehall FCO building's attempt to accommodate the new influx of diplomatic papers—this effort, too, seems doomed to fail in the medium term. The heavy reliance on technology in UKUSA also leaves the working of the system vulnerable to various failures, such as the January 2000 power failure at the NSA, which shifted all analytic work to the British for three days. Material resources that are central to the coproduction of emergent agencies associated with geopolitical assemblages are therefore critical vulnerabilities.

Of course, these state apparatuses are aware of such vulnerabilities, and they work to improve the resilience of their systems when stressed.[18] The NATO and CFSP case studies each reflect different models of resilience. With regard to NATO interoperability, a rigorous process is in place to evaluate existing standards to ensure that there are no unexpected outcomes. Each STANAG is evaluated on a three-year cycle to identify any changes in its effects on military capabilities as, for instance, new equipment comes online (which may produce negative interactions with existing standards). As a result, officially, every STANAG works exactly as intended (of course, we should be skeptical of this claim). This is a highly labor-intensive system (and only more so as STANAGs proliferate over time). The CFSP case study reflects a different model of resilience in that the capacities of the individual member states remain intact and work alongside as well as through CFSP. Of course, truly collective action might be preferable, but European habits of political cooperation dating back to the mid-twentieth century might still have an effect even without the material resources of the EEAS.

All of this points to a dimension of power that this volume's emphasis on everyday diplomacy highlights perhaps better than other accounts of international relations: bureaucratic capacity. The case study of the nineteenth-century Foreign Office highlighted the crucial role of office space and its role in generating affective atmospheres of efficiency that were productive of diplomatic power. A well-resourced Foreign Office, both in terms of physical plant and human resources, was understood to result in more influence abroad. For UKUSA, the threatened budget cuts after World War II and the subsequent release of staff knowledgeable in decryption inspired the United States and the United Kingdom to club together in order to maintain current capabilities into the peacetime era. For NATO interoperability, the relative asymmetry of the member state's bureaucratic power means that the United States shepherds about 60 percent of the military alliance's standards through the process; this is a lever of power that is explicitly understood as such by those involved. Finally, the creation of the EEAS has provided bureaucratic power and diplomatic presence for many small European states in parts of the world where they would never otherwise prioritize their relatively scant diplomatic resources. In each of these cases, bureaucratic power—the ability to shuffle more paper, have redundant systems, and store archives—remains a key dimension of transnational "kingship" (see chap. 1). As such it is both a vulnerability and a source of resilience.

Approaching international relations through the lens of assemblage theory enables us to empirically consider specific geopolitical assemblages both as they are and as they might be. It therefore opens up new horizons for critical, empirical research that can direct our attention simultaneously to the everyday times and spaces in which international relations actually unfold and to the macroscaled patterns that both result from and simplify those local processes. It is incumbent on critical scholars to do more than deconstruct these simplifying accounts—we must counter them with new explanations that explain and enlighten.

Introduction

1. Charles Dickens, *A Tale of Two Cities* (Hertfordshire: Wordsworth Editions, 1999), 191.

2. Christopher Meyer, *DC Confidential*, new edn. (London: Weidenfeld and Nicolson, 2006).

3. Gearóid Ó Tuathail, "'Just Out Looking for a Fight': American Affect and the Invasion of Iraq," *Antipode* 35, no. 5 (2003): 856–70.

4. Colin Camerer, *Behavioral Game Theory: Experiments in Strategic Interaction* (Princeton: Princeton University Press, 2011).

5. Scott Burchill, *The National Interest in International Relations Theory* (Houndmills: Palgrave Macmillan, 2005).

6. Derald Wing Sue, *Microaggressions and Marginality: Manifestation, Dynamics, and Impact* (New York: John Wiley and Sons, 2010).

7. Jeremy W. Crampton and Stuart Elden, *Space, Knowledge and Power: Foucault and Geography* (Farnham, U.K.: Ashgate, 2007); Chris Philo, "Foucault's Geography," *Environment and Planning D: Society and Space* 10, no. 2 (1992): 137–61.

8. For feminist approaches, see Lorraine Dowler and Joanne Sharp, "A Feminist Geopolitics?," *Space and Polity* 5, no. 3 (2001): 165–76; Jennifer Hyndman, "Mind the Gap: Bridging Feminist and Political Geography through Geopolitics," *Political Geography* 23, no. 3 (2004): 307–22. On popular geopolitics, see Jason Dittmer and Klaus Dodds, "Popular Geopolitics Past and Future: Fandom, Identities and Audiences," *Geopolitics* 13, no. 3 (2008): 437–57; Jason Dittmer and Nicholas Gray, "Popular Geopolitics 2.0: Towards New Methodologies of the Everyday," *Geography Compass* 4, no. 11 (2010): 1664–77.

9. Katherine Brickell, "Geopolitics of Home," *Geography Compass* 6, no. 10 (2012): 575–88; Christopher Harker, "Spacing Palestine through the Home," *Transactions of the Institute of British Geographers* 34, no. 3 (2009): 320–32.

10. Merje Kuus, "Commentary: Europe and the Baroque." *Environment and Planning D: Society and Space* 28, no. 3 (2010): 383.

11. Timothy Mitchell, "The Limits of the State: Beyond Statist Approaches and Their Critics," *American Political Science Review* 85, no. 1 (1991): 77–96.

12. Neil Brenner, "The Limits to Scale? Methodological Reflections on Scalar Structuration," *Progress in Human Geography* 25, no. 4 (2001): 591–614; Andrew E. G. Jonas, "Pro Scale: Further Reflections on the 'Scale Debate' in Human Geography," *Transactions of the Institute of British Geographers* 31, no. 3 (2006): 399–406; Martin Jones, "Phase Space: Geography, Relational Thinking, and Beyond," *Progress in Human Geography* 33, no. 4 (2009): 487–506; Sallie A. Marston, John Paul Jones, and Keith Woodward, "Human Geography without Scale," *Transactions of the Institute of British Geographers* 30, no. 4 (2005): 416–32; Roderick P. Neumann, "Political Ecology: Theorizing Scale," *Progress in Human Geography* 33, no. 3 (2009): 398–406.

13. Joe Painter, "Prosaic Geographies of Stateness," *Political Geography* 25, no. 7 (2006): 760.

14. Fiona McConnell, Terri Moreau, and Jason Dittmer, "Mimicking State Diplomacy: The Legitimizing Strategies of Unofficial Diplomacies," *Geoforum* 43, no. 4 (2012): 804–14.

15. Homi Bhabha, "Of Mimicry and Man: The Ambivalence of Colonial Discourse," *Discipleship* 28 (1984): 127.

16. Elaine K. Ginsberg, ed., *Passing and the Fictions of Identity* (Durham, NC: Duke University Press, 1996).

17. Pierre Bourdieu, *Outline of a Theory of Practice* (Cambridge: Cambridge University Press, 1977).

18. Alex Jeffrey, *The Improvised State: Sovereignty, Performance and Agency in Dayton Bosnia* (Chichester, U.K.: Wiley-Blackwell, 2012), 32, 35.

19. Pierre Bourdieu, *Distinction: A Social Critique of the Judgement of Taste* (London: Routledge, 2010); Pierre Bourdieu, *The Logic of Practice*, new edn. (Cambridge: Polity, 1992).

20. Merje Kuus, *Geopolitics and Expertise: Knowledge and Authority in European Diplomacy* (Chichester, U.K.: Wiley-Blackwell, 2014); Iver Neumann, "Returning Practice to the Linguistic Turn: The Case of Diplomacy," *Millennium* 31, no. 3 (2002): 627–51; Vincent Pouliot, "The Logic of Practicality: A Theory of Practice of Security Communities," *International Organization* 62, no. 2 (2008): 257–88; Peter Jackson, "Pierre Bourdieu, the 'Cultural Turn' and the Practice of International History," *Review of International Studies* 34, no. 1 (2008): 155–81; Rebecca Adler-Nissen, *Bourdieu in International Relations: Rethinking Key Concepts in IR* (London: Routledge, 2012); Alun Jones and Julian Clark, "Mundane Diplomacies for the Practice of European Geopolitics," *Geoforum* 62, no. 1 (2015): 1–12; Veit Bachmann, "Spaces of Interaction: Enactments of Sociospatial Relations and an Emerging EU Diplomacy in Kenya," *Territory, Politics, Governance* 4, no. 1 (2016): 75–96.

21. Jacqueline Best, "Bureaucratic Ambiguity," *Economy and Society* 41, no. 1 (2012): 84–106.

22. Michele Acuto and Simon Curtis, *Reassembling International Theory: Assemblage Thinking and International Relations* (New York: Palgrave Macmillan, 2013).

23. Vincent Poulliot, "The Materials of Practice: Nuclear Warheads, Rhetorical Commonplaces and Committee Meetings in Russian–Atlantic Relations," *Cooperation and Conflict* 45, no. 3 (2010): 294–311; Christian Bueger, "Making Things Known: Epistemic Practices, the United Nations, and the Translation of Piracy," *International Political Sociology* 9 (2015): 1–18.

24. Jane Bennett, *Vibrant Matter: A Political Ecology of Things* (Durham, NC: Duke University Press, 2010). On imputing an essential power to objects in and of themselves, see Derek Gregory, "The Natures of War," *Antipode* 48, no. 1 (2016): 3–56; Eva Herschinger, "The Drug Dispositif: Ambivalent Materiality and the Addiction of the Global Drug Prohibition Regime," *Security Dialogue* 46, no. 2 (2015): 183–201.

25. Katharine Meehan, Ian Graham Ronald Shaw, and Sallie A. Marston, "Political Geographies of the Object," *Political Geography* 33 (2013): 1–10.

26. Thomas Lemke, "New Materialisms: Foucault and the 'Government of Things,'" *Theory, Culture and Society* 32, no. 4 (2015): 3–25.

27. Vicki Squire, "Desert 'Trash': Posthumanism, Border Struggles, and Humanitarian Politics," *Political Geography* 39 (2014): 11–21.

28. Meehan, Shaw, and Marston, "Political Geographies of the Object," 8, emphasis original.

29. Keith Woodward, "Affect, State Theory, and the Politics of Confusion," *Political Geography* 41 (2014): 21–31.

30. Martin Müller, "Assemblages and Actor-Networks: Rethinking Socio-Material Power, Politics and Space," *Geography Compass* 9, no. 1 (2015): 27–41.

31. Ben Anderson, Matthew Kearnes, Colin McFarlane, and Dan Swanton, "On Assemblages and Geography," *Dialogues in Human Geography* 2, no. 2 (2012): 171–89.

32. Manuel DeLanda, *A New Philosophy of Society: Assemblage Theory and Social Complexity* (London: Continuum, 2006), 12.

33. Elizabeth Grosz, *The Nick of Time: Politics, Evolution, and the Untimely* (Durham, NC: Duke University Press, 2004), 126.

34. Claire Rasmussen and Michael Brown, "The Body Politic as Spatial Metaphor," *Citizenship Studies* 9, no. 5 (2005): 469–84.

35. John Protevi, *Political Affect: Connecting the Social and the Somatic* (Minneapolis: University of Minnesota Press, 2009).

36. David Armstrong, "Globalization and the Social State," *Review of International Studies* 24, no. 4 (1998): 461–78.

37. Christian Wieland, "The Consequences of Early Modern Diplomacy: Entanglement, Discrimination, Mutual Ignorance—and State Building," in Antje Flüchter and Susann Richter, eds., *Structures on the Move: Technologies of Governance in Transcultural Encounter* (Heidelberg: Springer Science and Business Media, 2012), 271.

38. Noé Cornago, *Plural Diplomacies: Normative Predicaments and Functional Imperatives* (Leiden: Martinus Nijhoff, 2013), 40–41.

39. Francisco Aldecoa and Michael Keating, *Paradiplomacy in Action: The Foreign Relations of Subnational Governments* (Milton Park, U.K.: Psychology Press, 1999); Cornago, *Plural Diplomacies*.

40. Stuart Elden, "Governmentality, Calculation, Territory," *Environment and Planning D: Society and Space* 25, no. 3 (2007): 562–80.

41. Costas Constantinou, "Between Statecraft and Humanism: Diplomacy and Its Forms of Knowledge," *International Studies Review* 15, no. 2 (2013): 145.

42. Michel Foucault, *Security, Territory, Population: Lectures at the Collège de France*, trans. Graham Burchell, reprint edn. (Basingstoke: Palgrave Macmillan, 2009), 21.

43. Iver Neumann, *At Home with the Diplomats: Inside a European Foreign Ministry* (Ithaca: Cornell University Press, 2012).

44. Iver Neumann, *Diplomatic Sites: A Critical Inquiry* (Oxford: Oxford University Press, 2013).

45. I use the term *transnational* rather than *intergovernmental* to highlight both the blurring of the public and private within state assemblages and also the fact that some of these assemblages are not formalized in any way.

46. Paul Williams, "Who's Making UK Foreign Policy?," *International Affairs* 80, no. 5 (2004): 909–29.

47. Andrew Barry, *Political Machines: Governing a Technological Society* (London: Continuum, 2001).

48. Mary Mel French, *United States Protocol: The Guide to Official Diplomatic Etiquette* (Lanham, MD: Rowman and Littlefield, 2010).

49. Ian Buchanan, "Assemblage Theory and Its Discontents," *Deleuze Studies* 9, no. 3 (2015): 382–92.

50. N. Brenner, D. J. Madden, and D. Wachsmuth, "Assemblage Urbanism and the Challenges of Critical Urban Theory," *City* 15, no. 2 (2011): 225–40.

51. Graham Harman, *Prince of Networks: Bruno Latour and Metaphysics* (Melbourne: re.press, 2009).

52. Mark Salter, ed., *Making Things International 1: Circuits and Motion* (Minneapolis: University of Minnesota Press, 2015); Mark Salter, ed., *Making Things International 2: Catalysts and Reactions* (Minneapolis: University of Minnesota Press, 2016).

53. Didier Bigo, "Pierre Bourdieu and International Relations: Power of Practices, Practices of Power," *International Political Sociology* 5, no. 3 (2011): 225–58.

54. Erika Cudworth and Stephen Hobden, *Posthuman International Relations: Complexity, Ecologism and Global Politics* (New York: Zed, 2011), 10.

55. Lars-Erik Cederman, "Modeling the Size of Wars: From Billiard Balls to Sandpiles," *American Political Science Review* 97, no. 1 (2003): 135–50.

56. David Gress, *From Plato to NATO: The Idea of the West and Its Opponents* (New York: Free Press, 2004); Errol A. Henderson and Richard Tucker, "Clear and Present Strangers: The Clash of Civilizations and International Conflict," *International Studies Quarterly* 45, no. 2 (2001): 317–38; Samuel P. Huntington, "The Clash of Civilizations?," *Foreign Affairs* 72, no. 3 (1993): 22–49. On the

genealogy of the idea of civilizations, see Fernand Braudel, *A History of Civilizations* (New York: Penguin, 1995); Shmuel Noah Eisenstadt, *Comparative Civilizations and Multiple Modernities* (Leiden: Brill, 2003); Felipe Fernandez-Armesto, *Civilizations: Culture, Ambition, and the Transformation of Nature* (New York: Simon and Schuster, 2001); William H. McNeill, *The Rise of the West: A History of the Human Community, with a Retrospective Essay* (Chicago: University of Chicago Press, 1992).

57. Patrick Thaddeus Jackson, "'Civilization' on Trial," *Millennium* 28, no. 1 (1999): 142.

58. Jason Dittmer, "NATO, the EU and Central Europe: Differing Symbolic Shapes in Newspaper Accounts of Enlargement," *Geopolitics* 10, no. 1 (2005): 76–98; Iver B. Neumann, *Uses of the Other: "The East" in European Identity Formation* (Minneapolis: University of Minnesota Press, 1998).

59. Peter J. Hugill, *World Trade since 1431: Geography, Technology, and Capitalism* (Baltimore: Johns Hopkins University Press, 1995).

60. James C. Bennett, *The Anglosphere Challenge: Why the English-Speaking Nations Will Lead the Way in the Twenty-First Century*, new edn. (Lanham, MD: Rowman and Littlefield, 2007); Robert Conquest, "Toward an English-Speaking Union," *National Interest*, no. 57 (1999): 64–70.

61. Srdjan Vucetic, "Bound to Follow? The Anglosphere and U.S.-Led Coalitions of the Willing, 1950–2001," *European Journal of International Relations* 17, no. 1 (2011): 27–49.

62. Nick Megoran, "Neoclassical Geopolitics," *Political Geography* 29, no. 4 (2010): 188.

63. Srdjan Vucetic, *The Anglosphere: A Genealogy of a Racialized Identity in International Relations* (Stanford: Stanford University Press, 2011).

64. Edward Said, "The Clash of Ignorance," *The Nation*, 22 October 2001, https://www.thenation.com/article/clash-ignorance/.

65. Colin McFarlane, "On Context: Assemblage, Political Economy, and Structure," *City* 15, no. 3–4 (2011): 375–88.

66. Müller, "Assemblages and Actor-Networks," 33.

67. Ben Anderson and Colin McFarlane, "Assemblage and Geography," *Area* 43, no. 2 (2011): 125, emphasis added.

68. Martin Müller, "Opening the Black Box of the Organization: Socio-Material Practices of Geopolitical Ordering," *Political Geography* 31, no. 6 (2012): 382–83.

69. Cudworth and Hobden, *Posthuman International Relations*, 75.

70. Duncan Snidal, "Rational Choice and International Relations," in Walter Carlsnaes, Thomas Risse, and Beth A. Simmons, eds., *Handbook of International Relations* (London: Sage, 2002), 73–94.

71. Jennifer Sims, "Foreign Intelligence Liaison: Devils, Deals, and Details," *International Journal of Intelligence and Counterintelligence* 19, no. 2 (2006): 195–217; H. Bradford Westerfield, "America and the World of Intelligence Liaison," *Intelligence and National Security* 11, no. 3 (1996): 523–60; Stéphane Lefebvre, "The Difficulties and Dilemmas of International Intelligence Cooperation,"

International Journal of Intelligence and Counterintelligence 16, no. 4 (2003): 527–42; Chris Clough, "Quid Pro Quo: The Challenges of International Strategic Intelligence Cooperation," *International Journal of Intelligence and Counterintelligence* 17, no. 4 (2004): 601–13.

72. Eric Larson, *Interoperability of U.S. and NATO Allied Air Forces: Supporting Data and Case Studies* (Santa Monica: Rand Corporation, 2003); Terry Moon, Suzanne Fewell, and Hayley Reynolds, "The What, Why, When and How of Interoperability," *Defense and Security Analysis* 24, no. 1 (2008): 5–17; Raymond Millen, *Tweaking NATO: The Case for Integrated Multinational Divisions* (Colingdale, PA: Diane Publishing, 2002).

73. Paul James Cardwell, *EU External Relations and Systems of Governance: The CFSP, Euro-Mediterranean Partnership and Migration* (London: Routledge, 2013); Youri Devuyst, "The European Council and the CFSP after the Lisbon Treaty," *European Foreign Affairs Review* 17, no. 3 (2012): 327–49; Simon Duke and Sophie Vanhoonacker, "Administrative Governance in the CFSP: Development and Practice," *European Foreign Affairs Review* 11, no. 2 (2006): 163–82; Gisela Muller-Brandeck-Bocquet, "The New CFSP and ESDP Decision-Making System of the European Union," *European Foreign Affairs Review* 7, no. 3 (2002): 257–82; John Peterson and Helene Sjursen, *A Common Foreign Policy for Europe? Competing Visions of the CFSP* (London: Routledge, 2005); Steven Robinson, "Painting the CFSP in National Colours: Portuguese Strategies to Help Shape the EU's External Relations," *International Journal of Iberian Studies* 28, nos. 2–3 (2015): 235–55; Bernhard Stahl, Henning Boekle, Jorg Nadoll, and Anna Johannesdottir, "Understanding the Atlanticist-Europeanist Divide in the CFSP: Comparing Denmark, France, Germany and the Netherlands," *European Foreign Affairs Review* 9, no. 3 (2004): 417–41.

74. Nick J. Fox and Pam Alldred, "New Materialist Social Inquiry: Designs, Methods and the Research-Assemblage," *International Journal of Social Research Methodology* 18, no. 4 (2015): 400.

75. Fox and Alldred, "New Materialist Social Inquiry," 411.

76. Claudia Aradau and Jef Huysmans, "Critical Methods in International Relations: The Politics of Techniques, Devices and Acts," *European Journal of International Relations* 20, no. 3 (2014): 603.

77. Aradau and Huysmans, "Critical Methods in International Relations," 609.

78. Anja Kanngieser, "Geopolitics and the Anthropocene: Five Propositions for Sound," *GeoHumanities* 1, no. 1 (2015): 80–85.

79. William E. Connolly, *Neuropolitics: Thinking, Culture, Speed* (Minneapolis: University of Minnesota Press, 2002).

80. Kuus, *Geopolitics and Expertise.*

81. See Neumann, *At Home with the Diplomats.*

82. Müller, "Opening the Black Box of the Organization," 383.

83. See Cynthia Enloe, *Bananas, Beaches and Bases: Making Feminist Sense of International Politics* (London: Pandora, 1989).

One. Materializing Diplomacy

This chapter is based on research originally published in Jason Dittmer, "Theorizing a More-than-Human Diplomacy: Assembling the British Foreign Office, 1839–1874," *The Hague Journal of Diplomacy* 11, no. 1 (2016): 78–104.

1. Jon Coaffee, Paul O'Hare, and Marian Hawkesworth, "The Visibility of (In)Security: The Aesthetics of Planning Urban Defences against Terrorism," *Security Dialogue* 40, nos. 4–5 (2009): 489–511; Jane Loeffler, "Embassy Design: Security vs. Openness," *Foreign Service Journal* 82, no. 1 (2005): 44–51.
2. Andrew Vincent, *Theories of the State* (New York: Wiley-Blackwell, 1991).
3. R. B. J. Walker, *Inside/Outside: International Relations as Political Theory* (Cambridge: Cambridge University Press, 1993).
4. Anthony Seldon, *The Foreign Office: An Illustrated History of the Place and Its People* (London: HarperCollinsIllustrated, 2000), 39.
5. Edward Hertslet, *Recollections of the Old Foreign Office* (London: John Murray, 1901).
6. Seldon, *The Foreign Office*, 42.
7. Seldon, *The Foreign Office*, 39.
8. Jonathan Darling, "Another Letter from the Home Office: Reading the Material Politics of Asylum," *Environment and Planning D: Society and Space* 32, no. 3 (2014): 484–500; Florian Weisser, "Practices, Politics, Performativities: Documents in the International Negotiations on Climate Change," *Political Geography* 40, nos. A1–A2 (2014): 46–55.
9. Paul Adams, "Networks of Early Writing," *Historical Geography* 38 (2010): 71.
10. Costas Constantinou, *On the Way to Diplomacy* (Minneapolis: University of Minnesota Press, 1996), 77.
11. Peter Burger, *Charles Fenerty and His Paper Invention* (Toronto: PB Publishing, 2007).
12. Miles Ogborn, *Indian Ink: Script and Print in the Making of the English East India Company* (Chicago: University of Chicago Press, 2007).
13. *Report from Select Committee on Public Offices (Downing-Street)* (London: Her Majesty's Stationery Office, 1839), 28.
14. *Report from Select Committee on Public Offices (Downing-Street)*, 14.
15. Hertslet, *Recollections of the Old Foreign Office*.
16. *Report from the Select Committee on Foreign Office Reconstruction* (London: Her Majesty's Stationery Office, 1858).
17. Andrew Barry, *Material Politics: Disputes along the Pipeline* (New York: Wiley, 2013), 183.
18. *Report from Select Committee on Public Offices (Downing-Street)*, 1–2.
19. *Report from Select Committee on Public Offices (Downing-Street)*.
20. *Report from Select Committee on Public Offices (Downing-Street)*, 3.
21. *Report from Select Committee on Public Offices (Downing-Street)*, 5–6.
22. Seldon, *The Foreign Office*, 41.

23. Peter Kraftl and Peter Adey, "Architecture/Affect/Inhabitation: Geographies of Being-In Buildings," *Annals of the Association of American Geographers* 98, no. 1 (2008): 227.

24. Michel Foucault, *Security, Territory, Population: Lectures at the Collège de France*, translated by Graham Burchell, reprint edn. (Basingstoke: Palgrave Macmillan, 2009), 18.

25. *Report from Select Committee on Public Offices (Downing-Street)*, 14.

26. *Report from the Select Committee on Foreign Office Reconstruction*, 5.

27. *Report from the Select Committee on Foreign Office Reconstruction*, 2.

28. *Report from the Select Committee on Foreign Office Reconstruction*, 4.

29. *Report from the Select Committee on Foreign Office Reconstruction*.

30. Felix Driver, "Moral Geographies: Social Science and the Urban Environment in Mid-Nineteenth Century England," *Transactions of the Institute of British Geographers* 13, no. 3 (1988): 275–87.

31. *Report from the Select Committee on Foreign Office Reconstruction*, 58.

32. *Report from the Select Committee on Foreign Office Reconstruction*, 65.

33. Bernard Porter, *The Battle of the Styles: Society, Culture and the Design of a New Foreign Office, 1855–1861* (London: Continuum, 2011).

34. Ian Cobain, "Foreign Office Hoarding 1m Historic Files in Secret Archive," *Guardian*, 18 October 2013, http://www.theguardian.com/politics/2013/oct/18/foreign-office-historic-files-secret-archive.

35. Costas Constantinou, "Between Statecraft and Humanism: Diplomacy and Its Forms of Knowledge," *International Studies Review* 15, no. 2 (2013): 141–62.

36. William E. Connolly, *A World of Becoming* (Durham, NC: Duke University Press, 2010), 164.

37. Zara S. Steiner, *The Foreign Office and Foreign Policy, 1898–1914* (Cambridge: Cambridge University Press, 1969), 14.

38. Geoffrey Pigman, *Contemporary Diplomacy* (London: Polity, 2010).

Two. UKUSA Signals Intelligence Cooperation

This chapter is based on research originally published in Jason Dittmer, "Everyday Diplomacy: UKUSA Intelligence Cooperation and Geopolitical Assemblages," *Annals of the Association of American Geographers* 105, no. 3 (2015): 604–19.

1. See chapter 1.

2. Alan Turing, "Report on Cryptographic Machinery Available at Navy Department Washington," 28 November 1942, http://www.turing.org.uk/sources/washington.

3. Early papers concerning the U.K.–U.S. agreements, 8 July 1940–24 April 1944, n.d., https://www.nsa.gov/news-features/declassified-documents/ukusa/assets/files/early_papers_1940-1944.pdf.

4. Richard Aldrich, GCHQ: *The Uncensored Story of Britain's Most Secret Agency* (London: HarperPress, 2010).

5. Early papers concerning the U.K.–U.S. agreements, 8 July 1940–24 April 1944, n.d., https://www.nsa.gov/news-features/declassified-documents/ukusa/assets/files/early_papers_1940-1944.pdf.

6. Liaison in Far East with Foreign Intelligence Services, 16 April 1946, CI00096, National Security Archive, George Washington University, Washington, D.C.

7. Memo regarding an agreement between the U.S. Army and British GCCS concerning cooperation in matters relating to communication intelligence, 23 June 1943, Comms_int_23jun43, National Security Archive, George Washington University, Washington, D.C.

8. Aldrich, GCHQ.

9. Minutes of the 16th Meeting of the Army-Navy Cryptanalytic Research and Development Committee, 17 October 1945, HN00099, National Security Archive, George Washington University, Washington, D.C.

10. Peter Adey and Ben Anderson, "Anticipating Emergencies: Technologies of Preparedness and the Matter of Security," *Security Dialogue* 43, no. 2 (2012): 99–117.

11. Alasdair Pinkerton and Klaus Dodds, "Radio Geopolitics: Broadcasting, Listening and the Struggle for Acoustic Spaces," *Progress in Human Geography* 33, no. 1 (2009): 10–27.

12. L. Denfeld to CINCPAC, 4 March 1947, CI00211, National Security Archive, George Washington University, Washington, D.C.

13. J. Wenger to F-20, 21 May 1945, HN00019, p. 1, National Security Archive, George Washington University, Washington, D.C.

14. C. Cooke and Adm. King, 4 June 1945, HN00025, p. 1, National Security Archive, George Washington University, Washington, D.C.

15. J. Wenger to F-20, 21 May 1945, HN00019, p. 2, National Security Archive, George Washington University, Washington, D.C.

16. H. Thebaud and Adm. King, 4 June 1945, HN00026, National Security Archive, George Washington University, Washington, D.C.

17. These code words changed over time, but I retain the terms *cream* and *ivory* for the sake of clarity.

18. Appendix A to British-U.S. C.I. Agreement, 26 February 1946, HW 80/3, p. 7, National Archives, London.

19. Appendix A to British-U.S. C.I. Agreement, 26 February 1946, HW 80/3, pp. 40–41, National Archives, London.

20. Appendix B: Principles of Security and Dissemination, 19 March 1953, HW 80/10, p. 7, National Archives, London.

21. Appendix B: Principles of Security and Dissemination, 19 March 1953, HW 80/10, National Archives, London.

22. Appendix B: Principles of Security and Dissemination, 19 March 1953, HW 80/10, p. 9, National Archives, London.

23. Enclosure A: Draft Agreement Proposed by ANCIB-ANCICC, 24 October 1945, HW 80/1, p. 6, National Archives, London.

24. Sir Stephen Lander, "International Intelligence Cooperation: An Inside Perspective," *Cambridge Review of International Affairs* 17, no. 3 (2004): 481–93.

25. Communications intelligence, 8 February 1946, p. 1, http://www.nsa.gov /news-features/declassified-documents/ukusa/assets/files/comms_int _8feb46.pdf.

26. Nigel Thrift and Andrew Leyshon, "A Phantom State? The De-Traditionalization of Money, the International Financial System and International Financial Centres," *Political Geography* 13, no. 4 (1994): 299–327.

27. Appendix to British-U.S. C.I. Agreement, 5 February 1946, HW 80/3, p. 6, National Archives, London.

28. Interviewee A, anonymous senior U.K. intelligence official (retired), interview by author, 2014.

29. Interviewee B, anonymous senior U.K. intelligence official (retired), interview by author, 2014.

30. Interviewee C, anonymous senior U.S. intelligence official (retired), interview by author, 2014.

31. Appendix G: Liaison and Channels for Exchange, 26 February 1946, pp. 1–2, HW 80/3, National Archives, London.

32. Interviewee B, anonymous senior U.K. intelligence official (retired), interview by author, 2014.

33. Memorandum: U.S.–British R.I. ("BRUSA") Circuit, 1944, https://www.nsa .gov/news-features/declassified-documents/ukusa/assets/files/brusa_7jan44 .pdf; U.S.–British R.I. ("BRUSA") Circuit: Instructions for Use, 1944, https:// www.nsa.gov/news-features/declassified-documents/ukusa/assets/files /brusa_14mar44.pdf.

34. Technical Conference for the Implementation of the U.S.–British Communications Intelligence Agreement, 11–27 March 1946, HW 80/6, National Archives, London.

35. Appendix H: Communications, 19 March 1953, HW 80/10, p. 1, National Archives, London.

36. Patrick Keefe, *Chatter: Uncovering the ECHELON Surveillance Network and the Secret World of Global Eavesdropping* (New York: Random House, 2006).

37. Duncan Campbell, Cahal Milmo, Kim Sengupta, Nigel Morris, and Tony Patterson, "Revealed: Britain's 'Secret Listening Post in the Heart of Berlin,'" *Independent*, 5 November 2013, http://www.independent.co.uk/news/uk/ home-news/revealed-britains-secret-listening-post-in- the-heart-of-berlin -8921548.html.

38. Glenn Greenwald, *No Place to Hide: Edward Snowden, the NSA and the Surveillance State* (London: Hamish Hamilton, 2014).

39. Greenwald, *No Place to Hide*, 94.

40. Greenwald, *No Place to Hide*, 94.

41. Greenwald, *No Place to Hide*, 98, emphasis original.

42. Nicky Hager, *Secret Power: New Zealand's Role in the International Spy Network* (Nelson, New Zealand: Craig Potton, 1996).

43. Kashmir Hill, "Blueprints of NSA's Ridiculously Expensive Data Center in Utah Suggest It Holds Less Info than Thought," *Forbes*, 24 July 2013, http://www .forbes.com/sites/kashmirhill/2013/07/24/blueprints-of-nsa-data-center-in -utah- suggest-its-storage-capacity-is-less-impressive-than-thought/.

44. Adam Svendsen, "The Globalization of Intelligence since 9/11: Frameworks and Operational Parameters," *Cambridge Review of International Affairs* 21, no. 1 (2008): 139.

45. Jeremy Crampton, Sue Roberts, and Ate Poorthuis, "The New Political Economy of Geographical Intelligence," *Annals of the Association of American Geographers* 104, no. 1 (2014): 196–214.

46. Greenwald, *No Place to Hide*, 168.

47. Interviewee D, anonymous senior U.S. intelligence official (retired), interview by author, 2014.

48. Interviewee A, anonymous senior U.K. intelligence official (retired), interview by author, 2014.

49. C. Snyder to Secretary of the Navy, 13 July 1945, HN00043, p. 3, National Security Archive, George Washington University, Washington, D.C.

50. Matthew Aid, *The Secret Sentry: The Untold History of the National Security Agency* (London: Bloomsbury, 2009), 3.

51. J. Wenger to F-20, 14 May 1945, HN00015, National Security Archive, George Washington University, Washington, D.C.

52. Enclosure A: Draft Agreement Proposed by ANCIB-ANCICC, 24 October 1945, HW 80/1, National Archives, London.

53. Lorna Lloyd, "'Us and Them': The Changing Nature of Commonwealth Diplomacy, 1880–1973," *Commonwealth and Comparative Politics* 39, no. 3 (2001): 9–30.

54. Draft British–U.S. Communication Intelligence Agreement, 1 November 1945, https://www.nsa.gov/news-features/declassified-documents/ukusa/assets/files/joint_mtg_1nov45.pdf.

55. Minutes of inauguration meeting of U.S.–British Signal Intelligence technical conference, 11 March 1946, HW 80/5, National Archives, London.

56. Minutes of inauguration meeting of U.S.–British Signal Intelligence technical conference, 11 March 1946, HW 80/5, National Archives, London.

57. Keefe, *Chatter*; Aid, *The Secret Sentry*.

58. Aldrich, GCHQ.

59. Memorandum on Post-War Plans for Intelligence and Counter-Intelligence, 3 November 1945, HN00105, p. 1, National Security Archive, George Washington University, Washington, D.C.

60. Aldrich, GCHQ, 93.

61. Christopher Andrew, "The Growth of the Australian Intelligence Community and the Anglo-American Connection," *Intelligence and National Security* 4, no. 2 (1989): 213–56.

62. Aldrich, GCHQ, 278.

63. Lander, "International Intelligence Cooperation," 487.

64. John Dumbrell, "Working with Allies: The United States, the United Kingdom, and the War on Terror," *Politics and Policy* 34, no. 2 (2006): 461.

65. Aldrich, GCHQ.

66. Interviewee B, anonymous senior U.K. intelligence official (retired), interview by author, 2014.

67. Robert Kaiser, "The Birth of Cyberwar," *Political Geography* 46 (2015): 11–20.
68. Minutes of inauguration meeting of U.S.–British Signal Intelligence technical conference, 11 March 1946, HW 80/5, p. 1, National Archives, London.
69. Interviewee A, anonymous senior U.K. intelligence official (retired), interview by author, 2014.

Three. Interoperability and Standardization

1. BJSM Washington to Ministry of Defence, London, 22 January 1951, FO 371/965567/2, National Archives, London.
2. BJSM Washington to Ministry of Defence, London, 29 August 1951, FO 371/96561, National Archives, London.
3. The British ended up making it physically impossible to set their FN rifles to fully automatic, as the bullets made it ineffective. See Appendix A, 27 June 1957, DEFE 7/1613/16, National Archives, London.
4. Memo from P. H. Moberly, 29 October 1951, FO 371/96562/1, National Archives, London.
5. "The problem of standardization is really one which must be decided by military experts. In the case of .30 versus .28 ammunition, it is probably too late for either us or the Americans to change. On purely NATO grounds it is a pity that our experts have not been able to accept the .30 rifle, for there could then have been a standard SAA for all purposes of NATO production and equipment." Memo from P. H. Moberly, 29 October 1951, FO 371/96562/1, National Archives, London.
6. The T44 and FN Rifles, 21 May 1957, DEFE 7/1613/7, National Archives, London.
7. NATO, *Backgrounder: Interoperability for Joint Operations* (Brussels: NATO Public Diplomacy Division, 2006).
8. Manuel DeLanda, *A New Philosophy of Society: Assemblage Theory and Social Complexity* (London: Continuum, 2006), 10.
9. John Barry and James Blaker, "After the Storm: The Growing Convergence of the Air Force and the Navy," *Naval War College Review* 54, no. 4 (2001): 117–33.
10. Virginie Mamadouh and Hermann van der Wusten, "The Footprint of the JSF/F-35 Lightning II Military Jet in the Netherlands: Geopolitical and Geoeconomic Considerations in Arms Procurement and Arms Production," *L'Espace Politique* 15 (2011), http://espacepolitique.revues.org/2124.
11. NATO, *Backgrounder*, 3.
12. Cesare Balducci, NATO Standardization Agency, interview by author, 15 March 2014.
13. Cornelious Doraton, U.S. Army, interview by author, 21 March 2014.
14. NATO, *NATO Standardization Agency*, 3d edn. (Brussels: NATO, n.d.). Note that MAS was originally named the Military Standardization Agency (MSA) but was renamed in the same year it was founded. MAS was moved to Brussels in 1970.
15. Memorandum for the Members of the Military Committee in Permanent Session, 3 December 1963, MC 20/5, NATO Archives, Brussels.

16. North Atlantic Military Committee Decision on MC 20/2, 7 December 1954, MC 20/2, NATO Archives, Brussels.

17. Memorandum for the Members of the Military Committee in Chiefs of Staff Session, 24 November 1980, IMSM-CBX-496–80 (Revised), p. 3, NATO Archives, Brussels.

18. Memorandum for the Members of the Military Committee in Chiefs of Staff Session, 24 November 1980, IMSM-CBX-496–80 (Revised), p. 3, NATO Archives, Brussels.

19. Memorandum for the Members of the Military Committee in Chiefs of Staff Session, 24 November 1980, IMSM-CBX-496–80 (Revised), p. 7, NATO Archives, Brussels.

20. Enclosure 1, 29 April 1981, IMSWM-124–81, p. 5, NATO Archives, Brussels.

21. Memorandum for the Members of the Military Committee in Chiefs of Staff Session, 24 November 1980, IMSM-CBX-496–80 (Revised), p. 5, NATO Archives, Brussels.

22. *Production, Maintenance and Management of NATO Standardization Documents*, 2011, edition J, version 2, AAP-03(j)(2)e, NATO Archives, Brussels.

23. Cesare Balducci, NATO Standardization Agency, interview by author, 15 March 2014.

24. Cesare Balducci, NATO Standardization Agency, interview by author, 15 March 2014.

25. Cesare Balducci, NATO Standardization Agency, interview by author, 15 March 2014.

26. These working groups, or the NSA as a whole, might be understood as an "infrastructural zone." Andrew Barry, "Technological Zones," *European Journal of Social Theory* 9, no. 2 (2006): 239–53.

27. Cesare Balducci, NATO Standardization Agency, interview by author, 15 March 2014.

28. Cornelious Doraton, U.S. Army, interview by author, 21 March 2014.

29. Cornelious Doraton, U.S. Army, interview by author, 21 March 2014.

30. I should note that security concerns in NATO headquarters precluded my ability to investigate this conviviality in more ethnographic fashion. However, being escorted around by my respondents allowed me to glimpse the truly multinational nature of these "water cooler" interactions, if only briefly.

31. Cesare Balducci, NATO Standardization Agency, interview by author, 15 March 2014.

32. Cesare Balducci, NATO Standardization Agency, interview by author, 15 March 2014.

33. *Production, Maintenance and Management of NATO Standardization Documents*, 2011, edition J, version 2, AAP-03(j)(2)e, p. 12, NATO Archives, Brussels, emphasis added.

34. Bruno Latour, *Science in Action* (Milton Keynes, U.K.: Open University Press, 1987).

35. *Production, Maintenance and Management of NATO Standardization Documents*, 2011, edition J, version 2, AAP-03(j)(2)e, p. 17, NATO Archives, Brussels.

36. *Production, Maintenance and Management of NATO Standardization Documents,* 2011, edition J, version 2, AAP-03(J)(2)e, p. 13, NATO Archives, Brussels.

37. Memorandum for the Working Group, 5 April 1954, SGWM-190–54, NATO Archives, Brussels.

38. North Atlantic Military Committee Decision on MC 20/2, 7 December 1954, MC 20/2, p. 6, NATO Archives, Brussels.

39. NATO, *Backgrounder,* 5.

40. NATO, *Backgrounder.*

41. NATO *Glossary of Standardization Terms and Definitions,* 2011, edition B, version 1, AAP-42(2011), NATO Archives, Brussels; NATO *Glossary of Abbreviations Used in NATO Documents and Publications,* 2013, AAP-15, NATO Archives, Brussels.

42. For details on negotiations of this STANAG, see WO 32/19326, National Archives, London.

43. Cesare Balducci, NATO Standardization Agency, interview by author, 15 March 2014.

44. John Protevi, *Political Affect: Between the Social and the Somatic* (Minneapolis: University of Minnesota Press, 2009).

45. BJSM Washington to Ministry of Defence, London, 11 May 1951, FO 371/96569/1, National Archives, London.

46. Of course, the fact that it was American-made surely factored in as well.

47. Sir Richard Powell, *Progress of Standardization,* 28 June 1957, DEFE 7/1613/18A, National Archives, London.

48. Draft of a suggested letter to Mr. A. Kershaw, MP, n.d., WO 32/17231/45A, National Archives, London.

49. Report by the Standardization Policy and Coordination Committee to the Standing Group on Establishment of a Military Standardization Agency of the North Atlantic Treaty Standing Group Organization, 22 August 1950, SG 39/3, p. 5, NATO Archives, Brussels.

50. Interoperability and Standardization of Equipment in NATO, 2 March 1978, DEFE 13/1167/E10, National Archives, London.

51. North Atlantic Military Committee Decision on MC 20/2, 7 December 1954, MC 20/2, p. 7, NATO Archives, Brussels.

52. Memorandum for Admiral M. Douguet, French Member, Standing Group, 3 June 1963, SGWM-051063, NATO Archives, London.

53. Standing Group Decision on S.G. 39/12, 30 March 1954, SG_039_12_FINAL, NATO Archives, Brussels.

54. Standing Group Decision on S.G. 39/12, 30 March 1954, SG_039_12_FINAL, p. 3, NATO Archives, Brussels.

55. Standing Group Decision on S.G. 39/12, 30 March 1954, SG_039_12_FINAL, p. 3, NATO Archives, Brussels.

56. North Atlantic Military Committee Decision on MC 20/2, 7 December 1954, MC 20/2, pp. 6–7, NATO Archives, Brussels.

57. V. Macklin, Interoperability and Standardization of Equipment with NATO, 20 January 1978, DEFE 13/1167/E1, National Archives, London.

58. Standardization and Interoperability within NATO, 20 February 1978, DEFE 13/1167/E6, National Archives, London.

59. Draft White Paper: Standardization in the Armed Forces, 22 October 1951, FO 371/96562/7, National Archives, London. Australia would later join the group.

60. Minute from I. C. Alexander, 18 March 1953, FO 371/108021, p. 2, National Archives, London.

61. Minute from R. Starkey, 14 December 1956, FO 371/124872/7, National Archives, London.

62. Search for a Framework for Cooperation and Trade in the Field of Armaments, 31 October 1975, FCO 41/1675, p. 112, National Archives, London.

63. International Interdependence Organizations, 13 February 1978, DEFE 13/1167/E9, National Archives, London.

64. Standardization of Weapons Systems (draft speech), n.d., DEFE 13/1167/E17, National Archives, London.

65. U.S. Congress, NATO *Standardization, Interoperability and Readiness: Report of the Special Subcommittee on NATO Standardization, Interoperability, and Readiness of the Committee on Armed Services, House of Representatives* (Washington: U.S. Government Printing Office, 1979). It should be noted that "interoperability and standardization" in this report refer to interoperability and standardization of war materiel, not of procedures.

66. Draft letter to Peter Wall, MP, 28 March 1978, DEFE 13/1167/E39, National Archives, London.

67. Interoperability and Standardization of Equipment in NATO, 2 March 1978, DEFE 13/1167/E41, National Archives, London.

68. I was shown this PowerPoint but not allowed to take a copy as it was for internal use only.

69. DeLanda, *A New Philosophy of Society*.

70. Cornelious Doraton, U.S. Army, interview by author, 21 March 2014.

71. Antonio Gramsci, *Prison Notebooks, Volume 3* (New York: Columbia University Press, 2011).

72. Cesare Balducci, NATO Standardization Agency, interview by author, 15 March 2014.

73. Cesare Balducci, NATO Standardization Agency, interview by author, 15 March 2014.

74. Celeste Wallander, "Institutional Assets and Adaptability: NATO after the Cold War," *International Organization* 54, no. 4 (2000): 705–35.

75. Cesare Balducci, NATO Standardization Agency, interview by author, 15 March 2014.

76. Cesare Balducci, NATO Standardization Agency, interview by author, 15 March 2014.

77. Cornelious Doraton, U.S. Army, interview by author, 21 March 2014.

Four. A Common Foreign and Security Policy

1. Julian Clark and Alun Jones, "Europeanization and Its Discontents," *Space and Polity* 13, no. 3 (2009): 193–212.

2. Elfriede Regelsberger, "EPC in the 1980s: Reaching Another Plateau?," in Alfred Pijpers, Elfriede Regelsberger, and Wolfgang Wessels, eds., *European Political Cooperation in the 1980s: A Common Foreign Policy for Western Europe?* (Dordrecht: Martinus Nijhoff, 1988), 3–48.

3. Regelsberger, "EPC in the 1980s."

4. Sir Stephen Wall, retired from the Foreign and Commonwealth Office and Cabinet Office, interview by author, 14 August 2014.

5. Sir Stephen Wall, retired from the Foreign and Commonwealth Office and Cabinet Office, interview by author, 14 August 2014.

6. Sir Stephen Wall, retired from the Foreign and Commonwealth Office and Cabinet Office, interview by author, 14 August 2014.

7. Regelsberger, "EPC in the 1980s."

8. Sir Stephen Wall, retired from the Foreign and Commonwealth Office and Cabinet Office, interview by author, 14 August 2014.

9. Regelsberger, "EPC in the 1980s."

10. Regelsberger, "EPC in the 1980s," 23–24.

11. Sir Brian Crowe, "A Common European Foreign Policy after Iraq?," in Martin Holland, ed., *Common Foreign and Security Policy: The First Ten Years*, 2d edn. (London: Continuum, 2005), 28–43.

12. David Spence, "The Early Days of the European External Action Service: A Practitioner's View," *The Hague Journal of Diplomacy* 7, no. 1 (2012): 115–34.

13. The Foreign Affairs Council is the name given to the Council of Ministers when it is dealing with foreign affairs and is populated by the member states' foreign ministers.

14. Sophie Vanhoonacker and Karolina Pomorska, "The European External Action Service and Agenda-Setting in European Foreign Policy," *Journal of European Public Policy* 20, no. 9 (2013): 1316–31.

15. Jackie Granger, EU Institute for Security Studies, interview by author, 22 March 2014; Alun Jones and Julian Clark, "Europeanisation and Discourse Building: The European Commission, European Narratives and European Neighbourhood Policy," *Geopolitics* 13, no. 3 (2008): 545–71.

16. Anonymous staffer, Political and Security Committee, EEAS, interview by author, 17 March 2014.

17. Federica Bicchi, "Information Exchanges, Diplomatic Networks and the Construction of European Knowledge in European Union Foreign Policy," *Cooperation and Conflict* 49, no. 2 (2014): 239–59.

18. Sir Stephen Wall, retired from the Foreign and Commonwealth Office and Cabinet Office, interview by author, 14 August 2014.

19. Interview respondent quoted in Magnus Ekengren, *The Time of European Governance* (Manchester: Manchester University Press, 2002), 79, emphasis added.

20. Ekengren, *The Time of European Governance.*

21. Anonymous staffer, Political and Security Committee, EEAS, interview by author, 17 March 2014.

22. Hugo Shorter, Foreign and Commonwealth Office, interview by author, 3 August 2014.

23. Veit Bachmann, research associate, Nairobi EEAS Delegation, interview by author, 22 September 2014.

24. Stephen Blockmans, Center for European Policy Studies, interview by author, 13 March 2014.

25. Ben Anderson and Rachel Gordon, "Government and (Non)Event: The Promise of Control," *Social and Cultural Geography*, DOI: 10.1080 /14649365.2016.1163727.

26. Ben Anderson, "Governing Emergencies: The Politics of Delay and the Logic of Response," *Transactions of the Institute of British Geographers* 41, no. 1 (2016): 14–26.

27. Robert Krengel, European Commission, interview by author, 17 March 2014.

28. Merje Kuus, "Bureaucracy and Place: Expertise in the European Quarter," *Global Networks* 11, no. 4 (2011): 421–39.

29. Robert Krengel, interview by author, 17 March 2014.

30. Zuzana Murdoch, Jarle Trondal, and Stefean Ganzle, "Building Foreign Affairs Capacity in the EU: The Recruitment of Member State Officials to the European External Action Service (EEAS)," *Public Administration* 92, no. 1 (2014): 71–86; Ana Juncos and Karolina Pomorska, "Manufacturing *Esprit de Corps*: The Case of the European External Action Service," *Journal of Common Market Studies* 52, no. 2 (2014): 302–19.

31. Veit Bachmann, research associate, Nairobi EEAS Delegation, interview by author, 22 September 2014.

32. Stephen Blockmans, Center for European Policy Studies, interview by author, 13 March 2014.

33. Veit Bachmann, research associate, Nairobi EEAS Delegation, interview by author, 22 September 2014.

34. For an excellent discussion of this in the EU context, see Merje Kuus, *Geopolitics and Expertise: Knowledge and Authority in European Diplomacy* (Chichester, U.K.: Wiley-Blackwell, 2014).

35. Hugo Shorter, Foreign and Commonwealth Office, interview by author, 3 August 2014.

36. Anonymous staffer, Political and Security Committee, EEAS, interview by author, 17 March 2014.

37. Anonymous staffer, Political and Security Committee, EEAS, interview by author, 17 March 2014.

38. Anonymous staffer, Political and Security Committee, EEAS, interview by author, 17 March 2014.

39. Anonymous staffer, Political and Security Committee, EEAS, interview by author, 17 March 2014.

40. Hugo Shorter, Foreign and Commonwealth Office, interview by author, 3 August 2014.

41. Hugo Shorter, Foreign and Commonwealth Office, interview by author, 3 August 2014.

42. Charles Tilly (1994), cited in Ekengren, *The Time of European Governance*, 10. See also Sami Moisio, Veit Bachmann, Luiza Bialasiewicz, Elena dell'Agnese,

Jason Dittmer, and Virginie Mamadouh, "Mapping the Political Geographies of Europeanization: National Discourses, External Perceptions and the Question of Popular Culture," *Progress in Human Geography* 37, no. 6 (2013): 737–61.

43. Hugo Shorter, Foreign and Commonwealth Office, interview by author, 3 August 2014.

44. Hugo Shorter, Foreign and Commonwealth Office, interview by author, 3 August 2014.

45. Sir Stephen Wall, retired from the Foreign and Commonwealth Office and Cabinet Office, interview by author, 14 August 2014.

46. Sir Stephen Wall, retired from the Foreign and Commonwealth Office and Cabinet Office, interview by author, 14 August 2014.

47. Stephen Blockmans, Center for European Policy Studies, interview by author, 13 March 2014.

48. Stephen Blockmans, Center for European Policy Studies, interview by author, 13 March 2014.

49. Stephen Blockmans, Center for European Policy Studies, interview by author, 13 March 2014.

50. Sir Stephen Wall, retired from the FCO and Cabinet Office, interview by author, 14 August 2014.

51. Sir Stephen Wall, retired from the FCO and Cabinet Office, interview by author, 14 August 2014.

52. Stephen Blockmans, Center for European Policy Studies, interview by author, 13 March 2014.

53. Hugo Shorter, Foreign and Commonwealth Office, interview by author, 3 August 2014.

54. Sir Stephen Wall, retired from the Foreign and Commonwealth Office and Cabinet Office, interview by author, 14 August 2014.

55. Hugo Shorter, Foreign and Commonwealth Office, interview by author, 3 August 2014.

56. Stephen Blockmans, Center for European Policy Studies, interview by author, 13 March 2014.

57. Veit Bachmann, "A Step Outside: Observations from the World's Youngest State," *Geography Compass* 7, no. 11: 782.

58. Bachmann, "A Step Outside," 783.

Conclusion

1. Ash Amin, "Spatialities of Globalisation," *Environment and Planning A* 34, no. 3 (2002): 385–99; Michael Kearney, "The Local and the Global: The Anthropology of Globalization and Transnationalism," *Annual Review of Anthropology* 24 (1995): 547–65; Barney Warf, *Time-Space Compression: Historical Geographies* (London: Routledge, 2008).

2. Philip H. Gordon, "Europe's Uncommon Foreign Policy," *International Security* 22, no. 3 (1998): 74–100; Karen E. Smith, *European Union Foreign Policy in a Changing World* (New York: Wiley, 2013).

3. John Dumbrell, "Working with Allies: The United States, the United Kingdom, and the War on Terror," *Politics and Policy* 34, no. 2 (2006): 461.

4. Srdjan Vucetic, "Bound to Follow? The Anglosphere and US-Led Coalitions of the Willing, 1950–2001," *European Journal of International Relations* 17, no. 1 (2011): 27–49.

5. Here I mean peace in the very narrow sense of non-Anglo-American intervention. The ongoing crisis in Syria can in no sense be described as peace.

6. John Protevi, *Political Affect: Connecting the Social and the Somatic* (Minneapolis: University of Minnesota Press, 2009).

7. Jane Bennett, *Vibrant Matter: A Political Ecology of Things* (Durham, NC: Duke University Press, 2010).

8. From the foreword to Mary Mel French, *United States Protocol: The Guide to Official Diplomatic Etiquette* (Lanham, MD: Rowman and Littlefield, 2010), xiv.

9. Charles Kozierok, *The TCP/IP Guide: A Comprehensive, Illustrated Internet Protocols Reference* (San Francisco: No Starch Press, 2005), 12.

10. Rob Kitchin and Martin Dodge, *Code/Space: Software and Everyday Life* (Boston: Massachusetts Institute of Technology Press, 2011).

11. Thomas Lansford, "Security and Marketshare: Bridging the Transatlantic Divide in the Defense Industry," *European Security* 10, no. 1 (2001): 1–21; Hugo Meijer, "Post–Cold War Trends in the European Defence Industry: Implications for Transatlantic Industrial Relations," *Journal of Contemporary European Studies* 18, no. 1 (2010): 63–77; Eliot Cohen, "NATO Standardization: The Perils of Common Sense," *Foreign Policy*, no. 31 (1978): 72–90; Phillip Taylor, "Weapons Standardization in NATO: Collaborative Security or Economic Competition?," *International Organization* 36, no. 1 (1982): 95–112.

12. Anonymous Foreign and Commonwealth Office employee, Planning Unit, interview by author, n.d. On the diplomatic potential of social media, see Wilson P. Dizard, *Digital Diplomacy: U.S. Foreign Policy in the Information Age* (Westport, CT: Greenwood, 2001); Alec Ross, "Digital Diplomacy and US Foreign Policy," *The Hague Journal of Diplomacy* 6, nos. 3–4 (2011): 451–55; Lina Khatib, William Dutton, and Michael Thelwall, "Public Diplomacy 2.0: A Case Study of the U.S. Digital Outreach Team," *Middle East Journal* 66, no. 3 (2012): 453–72.

13. Interviewee B, anonymous senior U.K. intelligence official (retired), interview by author, 2014.

14. Interviewee C, anonymous senior U.S. intelligence official (retired), interview by author, 12 March 2014. Note that this account is contradicted in Nicky Hager, *Secret Power: New Zealand's Role in the International Spy Network* (Nelson, New Zealand: Craig Potton, 1996).

15. On one such transformation, see Dizard, *Digital Diplomacy*; Ross, "Digital Diplomacy and US Foreign Policy"; Khatib, Dutton, and Thelwall, "Public Diplomacy 2.0."

16. Iver Neumann, *At Home with the Diplomats: Inside a European Foreign Ministry* (Ithaca: Cornell University Press, 2012).
17. Iver Neumann, *At Home with the Diplomats*; Lorna Lloyd, "'Us and Them': The Changing Nature of Commonwealth Diplomacy, 1880–1973," *Commonwealth and Comparative Politics* 39, no. 3 (2001): 9–30.
18. Jonathan Pugh, "Resilience, Complexity and Post-Liberalism," *Area* 46, no. 3 (2014): 313–19; Kevin Grove, "Agency, Affect, and the Immunological Politics of Disaster Resilience," *Environment and Planning D: Society and Space* 32, no. 2 (2014): 240–56.

Acuto, Michele, and Simon Curtis. *Reassembling International Theory: Assemblage Thinking and International Relations*. New York: Palgrave Macmillan, 2013.

Adams, Paul. "Networks of Early Writing." *Historical Geography* 38 (2010): 70–89.

Adey, Peter, and Ben Anderson. "Anticipating Emergencies: Technologies of Preparedness and the Matter of Security." *Security Dialogue* 43, no. 2 (2012): 99–117.

Adler-Nissen, Rebecca. *Bourdieu in International Relations: Rethinking Key Concepts in IR*. London: Routledge, 2012.

Aid, Matthew. *The Secret Sentry: The Untold History of the National Security Agency*. London: Bloomsbury, 2009.

Aldecoa, Francisco, and Michael Keating. *Paradiplomacy in Action: The Foreign Relations of Subnational Governments*. Milton Park, U.K.: Psychology Press, 1999.

Aldrich, Richard. *GCHQ: The Uncensored Story of Britain's Most Secret Agency*. London: HarperPress, 2010.

Amin, Ash. "Spatialities of Globalisation." *Environment and Planning A* 34, no. 3 (2002): 385–99.

Anderson, Ben. "Governing Emergencies: The Politics of Delay and the Logic of Response." *Transactions of the Institute of British Geographers* 41, no. 1 (2016): 14–26.

Anderson, Ben, and Rachel Gordon. "Government and (Non)Event: The Promise of Control." *Social and Cultural Geography*. DOI: 10.1080/14649365.2016.1163727.

Anderson, Ben, Matthew Kearnes, Colin McFarlane, and Dan Swanton. "On Assemblages and Geography." *Dialogues in Human Geography* 2, no. 2 (2012): 171–89.

Anderson, Ben, and Colin McFarlane. "Assemblage and Geography." *Area* 43, no. 2 (2011): 124–27.

Andrew, Christopher. "The Growth of the Australian Intelligence Community and the Anglo-American Connection." *Intelligence and National Security* 4, no. 2 (1989): 213–56.

Aradau, Claudia, and Jef Huysmans. "Critical Methods in International Relations: The Politics of Techniques, Devices and Acts." *European Journal of International Relations* 20, no. 3 (2014): 596–619.

Armstrong, David. "Globalization and the Social State." *Review of International Studies* 24, no. 4 (1998): 461–78.

Bachmann, Veit. "Spaces of Interaction: Enactments of Sociospatial Relations and an Emerging EU Diplomacy in Kenya." *Territory, Politics, Governance* 4, no. 1 (2016): 75–96.

———. "A Step Outside: Observations from the World's Youngest State." *Geography Compass* 7, no. 11: 778–89.

Barry, Andrew. *Material Politics: Disputes along the Pipeline*. New York: Wiley, 2013.

———. *Political Machines: Governing a Technological Society*. London: Continuum, 2001.

———. "Technological Zones." *European Journal of Social Theory* 9, no. 2 (2006): 239–53.

Barry, John, and James Blaker. "After the Storm: The Growing Convergence of the Air Force and the Navy." *Naval War College Review* 54, no. 4 (2001): 117–33.

Bennett, James C. *The Anglosphere Challenge: Why the English-Speaking Nations Will Lead the Way in the Twenty-First Century*. New edn. Lanham, MD: Rowman and Littlefield, 2007.

Bennett, Jane. *Vibrant Matter: A Political Ecology of Things*. Durham, NC: Duke University Press, 2010.

Best, Jacqueline. "Bureaucratic Ambiguity." *Economy and Society* 41, no. 1 (2012): 84–106.

Bhabha, Homi. "Of Mimicry and Man: The Ambivalence of Colonial Discourse." *Discipleship* 28 (1984): 125–33.

Bicchi, Federica. "Information Exchanges, Diplomatic Networks and the Construction of European Knowledge in European Union Foreign Policy." *Cooperation and Conflict* 49, no. 2 (2014): 239–59.

Bigo, Didier. "Pierre Bourdieu and International Relations: Power of Practices, Practices of Power." *International Political Sociology* 5, no. 3 (2011): 225–58.

Bourdieu, Pierre. *Distinction: A Social Critique of the Judgement of Taste*. London: Routledge, 2010.

———. *The Logic of Practice*. New edn. Cambridge: Polity, 1992.

———. *Outline of a Theory of Practice*. Cambridge: Cambridge University Press, 1977.

Braudel, Fernand. *A History of Civilizations*. New York: Penguin, 1995.

Brenner, Neil. "The Limits to Scale? Methodological Reflections on Scalar Structuration." *Progress in Human Geography* 25, no. 4 (2001): 591–614.

Brenner, N., D. J. Madden, and D. Wachsmuth. "Assemblage Urbanism and the Challenges of Critical Urban Theory." *City* 15, no. 2 (2011): 225–40.

Brickell, Katherine. "Geopolitics of Home." *Geography Compass* 6, no. 10 (2012): 575–88.

Buchanan, Ian. "Assemblage Theory and Its Discontents." *Deleuze Studies* 9, no. 3 (2015): 382–92.

Bueger, Christian. "Making Things Known: Epistemic Practices, the United Nations, and the Translation of Piracy." *International Political Sociology* 9, no. 1 (2015): 1–18.

Burchill, Scott. *The National Interest in International Relations Theory*. Houndmills: Palgrave Macmillan, 2005.

Burger, Peter. *Charles Fenerty and His Paper Invention*. Toronto: PB Publishing, 2007.

Camerer, Colin. *Behavioral Game Theory: Experiments in Strategic Interaction*. Princeton: Princeton University Press, 2011.

Cardwell, Paul James. *EU External Relations and Systems of Governance: The CFSP, Euro-Mediterranean Partnership and Migration*. London: Routledge, 2013.

Cederman, Lars-Erik. "Modeling the Size of Wars: From Billiard Balls to Sand-piles." *American Political Science Review* 97, no. 1 (2003): 135–50.

Clark, Julian, and Alun Jones. "Europeanization and Its Discontents." *Space and Polity* 13, no. 3 (2009): 193–212.

Clough, Chris. "Quid Pro Quo: The Challenges of International Strategic Intel-ligence Cooperation." *International Journal of Intelligence and Counterintelligence* 17, no. 4 (2004): 601–13.

Coaffee, Jon, Paul O'Hare, and Marian Hawkesworth. "The Visibility of (In)Se-curity: The Aesthetics of Planning Urban Defences against Terrorism." *Security Dialogue* 40, nos. 4–5 (2009): 489–511.

Cohen, Eliot. "NATO Standardization: The Perils of Common Sense." *Foreign Policy*, no. 31 (1978): 72–90.

Connolly, William E. *Neuropolitics: Thinking, Culture, Speed*. Minneapolis: University of Minnesota Press, 2002.

———. *A World of Becoming*. Durham, NC: Duke University Press, 2010.

Conquest, Robert. "Toward an English-Speaking Union." *National Interest*, no. 57 (1999): 64–70.

Constantinou, Costas. "Between Statecraft and Humanism: Diplomacy and Its Forms of Knowledge." *International Studies Review* 15, no. 2 (2013): 141–62.

———. *On the Way to Diplomacy*. Minneapolis: University of Minnesota Press, 1996.

Cornago, Noé. *Plural Diplomacies: Normative Predicaments and Functional Impera-tives*. Leiden: Martinus Nijhoff, 2013.

Crampton, Jeremy W., and Stuart Elden. *Space, Knowledge and Power: Foucault and Geography*. Aldershot: Ashgate, 2007.

Crampton, Jeremy, Sue Roberts, and Ate Poorthuis. "The New Political Economy of Geographical Intelligence." *Annals of the Association of American Geographers* 104, no. 1 (2014): 196–214.

Crowe, Sir Brian. "A Common European Foreign Policy after Iraq?" *Common For-eign and Security Policy: The First Ten Years*, 2d edn., ed. Martin Holland, 28–43, London: Continuum, 2005.

Cudworth, Erika, and Stephen Hobden. *Posthuman International Relations: Com-plexity, Ecologism and Global Politics*. New York: Zed, 2011.

Darling, Jonathan. "Another Letter from the Home Office: Reading the Material Politics of Asylum." *Environment and Planning D: Society and Space* 32, no. 3 (2014): 484–500.

DeLanda, Manuel. *A New Philosophy of Society: Assemblage Theory and Social Complexity*. London: Continuum, 2006.

Devuyst, Youri. "The European Council and the CFSP after the Lisbon Treaty," *European Foreign Affairs Review* 17, no. 3 (2012): 327–49.

Dickens, Charles. *A Tale of Two Cities*. Hertfordshire: Wordsworth Editions, 1999.

Dittmer, Jason. "Everyday Diplomacy: UKUSA Intelligence Cooperation and Geopolitical Assemblages." *Annals of the Association of American Geographers* 105, no. 3 (2015): 604–19.

———. "NATO, the EU and Central Europe: Differing Symbolic Shapes in Newspaper Accounts of Enlargement." *Geopolitics* 10, no. 1 (2005): 76–98.

———. "Theorizing a More-than-Human Diplomacy: Assembling the British Foreign Office, 1839–1874." *The Hague Journal of Diplomacy* 11, no. 1 (2016): 78–104.

Dittmer, Jason, and Klaus Dodds. "Popular Geopolitics Past and Future: Fandom, Identities and Audiences." *Geopolitics* 13, no. 3 (2008): 437–57.

Dittmer, Jason, and Nicholas Gray. "Popular Geopolitics 2.0: Towards New Methodologies of the Everyday." *Geography Compass* 4, no. 11 (2010): 1664–77.

Dizard, Wilson P. *Digital Diplomacy: U.S. Foreign Policy in the Information Age*. Westport, CT: Greenwood, 2001.

Dowler, Lorraine, and Joanne Sharp. "A Feminist Geopolitics?" *Space and Polity* 5, no. 3 (2001): 165–76.

Driver, Felix. "Moral Geographies: Social Science and the Urban Environment in Mid-Nineteenth Century England." *Transactions of the Institute of British Geographers* 13, no. 3 (1988): 275–87.

Duke, Simon, and Sophie Vanhoonacker. "Administrative Governance in the CFSP: Development and Practice." *European Foreign Affairs Review* 11, no. 2 (2006): 163–82.

Dumbrell, John. "Working with Allies: The United States, the United Kingdom, and the War on Terror." *Politics and Policy* 34, no. 2 (2006): 452–72.

Eisenstadt, Shmuel Noah. *Comparative Civilizations and Multiple Modernities*. Leiden: Brill, 2003.

Ekengren, Magnus. *The Time of European Governance*. Manchester: Manchester University Press, 2002.

Elden, Stuart. "Governmentality, Calculation, Territory." *Environment and Planning D: Society and Space* 25, no. 3 (2007): 562–80.

Enloe, Cynthia. *Bananas, Beaches and Bases: Making Feminist Sense of International Politics*. London: Pandora, 1989.

Fernandez-Armesto, Felipe. *Civilizations: Culture, Ambition, and the Transformation of Nature*. New York: Simon and Schuster, 2001.

Foucault, Michel. *Security, Territory, Population: Lectures at the Collège de France*. Translated by Graham Burchell. Reprint edn. Basingstoke: Palgrave Macmillan, 2009.

Fox, Nick J., and Pam Alldred. "New Materialist Social Inquiry: Designs, Methods and the Research-Assemblage." *International Journal of Social Research Methodology* 18, no. 4 (2015): 399–414.

French, Mary Mel. *United States Protocol: The Guide to Official Diplomatic Etiquette.* Lanham, MD: Rowman and Littlefield, 2010.

Ginsberg, Elaine K., ed. *Passing and the Fictions of Identity.* Durham, NC: Duke University Press, 1996.

Gordon, Philip H. "Europe's Uncommon Foreign Policy." *International Security* 22, no. 3 (1998): 74–100.

Gramsci, Antonio. *Prison Notebooks, Volume 3.* New York: Columbia University Press, 2011.

Greenwald, Glenn. *No Place to Hide: Edward Snowden, the NSA and the Surveillance State.* London: Hamish Hamilton, 2014.

Gregory, Derek. "The Natures of War." *Antipode* 48, no. 1 (2016): 3–56.

Gress, David. *From Plato to NATO: The Idea of the West and Its Opponents.* New York: Free Press, 2004.

Grosz, Elizabeth. *The Nick of Time: Politics, Evolution, and the Untimely.* Durham, NC: Duke University Press, 2004.

Grove, Kevin. "Agency, Affect, and the Immunological Politics of Disaster Resilience." *Environment and Planning D: Society and Space* 32, no. 2 (2014): 240–56.

Hager, Nicky. *Secret Power: New Zealand's Role in the International Spy Network.* Nelson, New Zealand: Craig Potton, 1996.

Harker, Christopher. "Spacing Palestine through the Home." *Transactions of the Institute of British Geographers* 34, no. 3 (2009): 320–32.

Harman, Graham. *Prince of Networks: Bruno Latour and Metaphysics.* Melbourne: re.press, 2009.

Henderson, Errol A., and Richard Tucker. "Clear and Present Strangers: The Clash of Civilizations and International Conflict." *International Studies Quarterly* 45, no. 2 (2001): 317–38.

Herschinger, Eva. "The Drug Dispositif: Ambivalent Materiality and the Addiction of the Global Drug Prohibition Regime." *Security Dialogue* 46, no. 2 (2015): 183–201.

Hertslet, Edward. *Recollections of the Old Foreign Office.* London: John Murray, 1901.

Hugill, Peter J. *World Trade since 1431: Geography, Technology, and Capitalism.* Baltimore: Johns Hopkins University Press, 1995.

Huntington, Samuel P. "The Clash of Civilizations?" *Foreign Affairs* 72, no. 3 (1993): 22–49.

Hyndman, Jennifer. "Mind the Gap: Bridging Feminist and Political Geography through Geopolitics." *Political Geography* 23, no. 3 (2004): 307–22.

Jackson, Patrick Thaddeus. "'Civilization' on Trial." *Millennium* 28, no. 1 (1999): 141–53.

Jackson, Peter. "Pierre Bourdieu, the 'Cultural Turn' and the Practice of International History." *Review of International Studies* 34, no. 1 (2008): 155–81.

Jeffrey, Alex. *The Improvised State: Sovereignty, Performance and Agency in Dayton Bosnia.* Chichester, U.K.: Wiley-Blackwell, 2012.

Jonas, Andrew E. G. "Pro Scale: Further Reflections on the 'Scale Debate' in Human Geography." *Transactions of the Institute of British Geographers* 31, no. 3 (2006): 399–406.

Jones, Alun, and Julian Clark. "Europeanisation and Discourse Building: The European Commission, European Narratives and European Neighbourhood Policy." *Geopolitics* 13, no. 3 (2008): 545–71.

———. "Mundane Diplomacies for the Practice of European Geopolitics." *Geoforum* 62, no. 1 (2015): 1–12.

Jones, Martin. "Phase Space: Geography, Relational Thinking, and Beyond." *Progress in Human Geography* 33, no. 4 (2009): 487–506.

Juncos, Ana, and Karolina Pomorska. "Manufacturing *Esprit de Corps*: The Case of the European External Action Service." *Journal of Common Market Studies* 52, no. 2 (2014): 302–19.

Kaiser, Robert. "The Birth of Cyberwar." *Political Geography* 46 (2015): 11–20.

Kanngieser, Anja. "Geopolitics and the Anthropocene: Five Propositions for Sound." *GeoHumanities* 1, no. 1 (2015): 80–85.

Kearney, Michael. "The Local and the Global: The Anthropology of Globalization and Transnationalism." *Annual Review of Anthropology* 24 (1995): 547–65.

Keefe, Patrick. *Chatter: Uncovering the ECHELON Surveillance Network and the Secret World of Global Eavesdropping.* New York: Random House, 2006.

Khatib, Lina, William Dutton, and Michael Thelwall. "Public Diplomacy 2.0: A Case Study of the U.S. Digital Outreach Team." *Middle East Journal* 66, no. 3 (2012): 453–72.

Kitchin, Rob, and Martin Dodge. *Code/Space: Software and Everyday Life.* Boston: Massachusetts Institute of Technology Press, 2011.

Kozierok, Charles. *The TCP/IP Guide: A Comprehensive, Illustrated Internet Protocols Reference.* San Francisco: No Starch Press, 2005.

Kraftl, Peter, and Peter Adey. "Architecture/Affect/Inhabitation: Geographies of Being-In Buildings." *Annals of the Association of American Geographers* 98, no. 1 (2008): 213–31.

Kuus, Merje. "Bureaucracy and Place: Expertise in the European Quarter." *Global Networks* 11, no. 4 (2011): 421–39.

———. "Commentary: Europe and the Baroque." *Environment and Planning D: Society and Space* 28, no. 3 (2010): 381–87.

———. *Geopolitics and Expertise: Knowledge and Authority in European Diplomacy.* Chichester, U.K.: Wiley-Blackwell, 2014.

Lander, Sir Stephen. "International Intelligence Cooperation: An Inside Perspective." *Cambridge Review of International Affairs* 17, no. 3 (2004): 481–93.

Lansford, Thomas. "Security and Marketshare: Bridging the Transatlantic Divide in the Defense Industry." *European Security* 10, no. 1 (2001): 1–21.

Larson, Eric. *Interoperability of U.S. and NATO Allied Air Forces: Supporting Data and Case Studies.* Santa Monica: Rand Corporation, 2003.

Latour, Bruno. *Science in Action.* Milton Keynes, U.K.: Open University Press, 1987.

Lefebvre, Stéphane. "The Difficulties and Dilemmas of International Intelligence Cooperation." *International Journal of Intelligence and Counterintelligence* 16, no. 4 (2003): 527–42.

Lemke, Thomas. "New Materialisms: Foucault and the 'Government of Things.'" *Theory, Culture and Society* 32, no. 4 (2015): 3–25.

Lloyd, Lorna. "'Us and Them': The Changing Nature of Commonwealth Diplomacy, 1880–1973." *Commonwealth and Comparative Politics* 39, no. 3 (2001): 9–30.

Loeffler, Jane. "Embassy Design: Security vs. Openness." *Foreign Service Journal* 82, no. 1 (2005): 44–51.

Mamadouh, Virginie, and Hermann van der Wusten. "The Footprint of the JSF/F-35 Lightning II Military Jet in the Netherlands: Geopolitical and Geoeconomic Considerations in Arms Procurement and Arms Production." *L'Espace Politique* 15 (2011). http://espacepolitique.revues.org/2124.

Marston, Sallie A., John Paul Jones, and Keith Woodward. "Human Geography without Scale." *Transactions of the Institute of British Geographers* 30, no. 4 (2005): 416–32.

McConnell, Fiona, Terri Moreau, and Jason Dittmer. "Mimicking State Diplomacy: The Legitimizing Strategies of Unofficial Diplomacies." *Geoforum* 43, no. 4 (2012): 804–14.

McFarlane, Colin. "On Context: Assemblage, Political Economy, and Structure." *City* 15, no. 3–4 (2011): 375–88.

McNeill, William H. *The Rise of the West: A History of the Human Community, with a Retrospective Essay*. Chicago: University of Chicago Press, 1992.

Meehan, Katharine, Ian Graham Ronald Shaw, and Sallie A. Marston. "Political Geographies of the Object." *Political Geography* 33 (2013): 1–10.

Megoran, Nick. "Neoclassical Geopolitics." *Political Geography* 29, no. 4 (2010): 188.

Meijer, Hugo. "Post–Cold War Trends in the European Defence Industry: Implications for Transatlantic Industrial Relations." *Journal of Contemporary European Studies* 18, no. 1 (2010): 63–77.

Meyer, Christopher. *DC Confidential*. New edn. London: Weidenfeld and Nicolson, 2006.

Millen, Raymond. *Tweaking NATO: The Case for Integrated Multinational Divisions*. Colingdale, PA: Diane Publishing, 2002.

Mitchell, Timothy. "The Limits of the State: Beyond Statist Approaches and Their Critics." *American Political Science Review* 85, no. 1 (1991): 77–96.

Moisio, Sami, Veit Bachmann, Luiza Bialasiewicz, Elena dell'Agnese, Jason Dittmer, and Virginie Mamadouh. "Mapping the Political Geographies of Europeanization: National Discourses, External Perceptions and the Question of Popular Culture." *Progress in Human Geography* 37, no. 6 (2013): 737–61.

Moon, Terry, Suzanne Fewell, and Hayley Reynolds. "The What, Why, When and How of Interoperability." *Defense and Security Analysis* 24, no. 1 (2008): 5–17.

Müller, Martin. "Assemblages and Actor-Networks: Rethinking Socio-Material Power, Politics and Space." *Geography Compass* 9, no. 1 (2015): 27–41.

———. "Opening the Black Box of the Organization: Socio-Material Practices of Geopolitical Ordering." *Political Geography* 31, no. 6 (2012): 382–83.

Muller-Brandeck-Bocquet, Gisela. "The New CFSP and ESDP Decision-Making System of the European Union." *European Foreign Affairs Review* 7, no. 3 (2002): 257–82.

Murdoch, Zuzana, Jarle Trondal, and Stefean Ganzle. "Building Foreign Affairs Capacity in the EU: The Recruitment of Member State Officials to the European External Action Service (EEAS)." *Public Administration* 92, no. 1 (2014): 71–86.

NATO. *Backgrounder: Interoperability for Joint Operations*. Brussels: NATO Public Diplomacy Division, 2006.

———. *NATO Standardization Agency*. 3d edn. Brussels: NATO, n.d.

Neumann, Iver. *At Home with the Diplomats: Inside a European Foreign Ministry*. Ithaca: Cornell University Press, 2012.

———. *Diplomatic Sites: A Critical Inquiry*. Oxford: Oxford University Press, 2013.

———. "Returning Practice to the Linguistic Turn: The Case of Diplomacy." *Millennium* 31, no. 3 (2002): 627–51.

———. *Uses of the Other: "The East" in European Identity Formation*. Minneapolis: University of Minnesota Press, 1998.

Neumann, Roderick P. "Political Ecology: Theorizing Scale." *Progress in Human Geography* 33, no. 3 (2009): 398–406.

Ogborn, Miles. *Indian Ink: Script and Print in the Making of the English East India Company*. Chicago: University of Chicago Press, 2007.

Ó Tuathail, Gearóid. "'Just Out Looking for a Fight': American Affect and the Invasion of Iraq." *Antipode* 35, no. 5 (2003): 856–70.

Painter, Joe. "Prosaic Geographies of Stateness." *Political Geography* 25, no. 7 (2006): 754–72.

Peterson, John, and Helene Sjursen. *A Common Foreign Policy for Europe? Competing Visions of the CFSP*. London: Routledge, 2005.

Philo, Chris. "Foucault's Geography." *Environment and Planning D: Society and Space* 10, no. 2 (1992): 137–61.

Pigman, Geoffrey. *Contemporary Diplomacy*. London: Polity, 2010.

Pinkerton, Alasdair, and Klaus Dodds. "Radio Geopolitics: Broadcasting, Listening and the Struggle for Acoustic Spaces." *Progress in Human Geography* 33, no. 1 (2009): 10–27.

Porter, Bernard. *The Battle of the Styles: Society, Culture and the Design of a New Foreign Office, 1855–1861*. London: Continuum, 2011.

Poulliot, Vincent. "The Logic of Practicality: A Theory of Practice of Security Communities." *International Organization* 62, no. 2 (2008): 257–88.

———. "The Materials of Practice: Nuclear Warheads, Rhetorical Commonplaces and Committee Meetings in Russian–Atlantic Relations." *Cooperation and Conflict* 45, no. 3 (2010): 294–311.

Protevi, John. *Political Affect: Connecting the Social and the Somatic*. Minneapolis: University of Minnesota Press, 2009.

Pugh, Jonathan. "Resilience, Complexity and Post-Liberalism." *Area* 46, no. 3 (2014): 313–19.

Rasmussen, Claire, and Michael Brown. "The Body Politic as Spatial Metaphor." *Citizenship Studies* 9, no. 5 (2005): 469–84.

Regelsberger, Elfriede. "EPC in the 1980s: Reaching Another Plateau?" *European Political Cooperation in the 1980s: A Common Foreign Policy for Western Europe?*, ed. Alfred Pijpers, Elfriede Regelsberger, and Wolfgang Wessels, 3–48. Dordrecht: Martinus Nijhoff, 1988.

Report from the Select Committee on Foreign Office Reconstruction. London: Her Majesty's Stationery Office, 1858.

Report from the Select Committee on Public Offices (Downing-Street). London: Her Majesty's Stationery Office, 1839.

Robinson, Steven. "Painting the CFSP in National Colours: Portuguese Strategies to Help Shape the EU's External Relations." *International Journal of Iberian Studies* 28, nos. 2–3 (2015): 235–55.

Ross, Alec. "Digital Diplomacy and U.S. Foreign Policy." *The Hague Journal of Diplomacy* 6, nos. 3–4 (2011): 451–55.

Salter, Mark, ed. *Making Things International 1: Circuits and Motion.* Minneapolis: University of Minnesota Press, 2015.

———. *Making Things International 2: Catalysts and Reactions.* Minneapolis: University of Minnesota Press, 2016.

Seldon, Anthony. *The Foreign Office: An Illustrated History of the Place and Its People.* London: HarperCollinsIllustrated, 2000.

Sims, Jennifer. "Foreign Intelligence Liaison: Devils, Deals, and Details." *International Journal of Intelligence and Counterintelligence* 19, no. 2 (2006): 195–217.

Smith, Karen E. *European Union Foreign Policy in a Changing World.* New York: Wiley, 2013.

Snidal, Duncan. "Rational Choice and International Relations." *Handbook of International Relations*, ed. Walter Carlsnaes, Thomas Risse, and Beth A. Simmons, 73–94. London: Sage, 2002.

Spence, David. "The Early Days of the European External Action Service: A Practitioner's View." *The Hague Journal of Diplomacy* 7, no. 1 (2012): 115–34.

Squire, Vicki. "Desert 'Trash': Posthumanism, Border Struggles, and Humanitarian Politics." *Political Geography* 39 (2014): 11–21.

Stahl, Bernhard, Henning Boekle, Jorg Nadoll, and Anna Johannesdottir. "Understanding the Atlanticist-Europeanist Divide in the CFSP: Comparing Denmark, France, Germany and the Netherlands." *European Foreign Affairs Review* 9, no. 3 (2004): 417–41.

Steiner, Zara S. *The Foreign Office and Foreign Policy, 1898–1914.* Cambridge: Cambridge University Press, 1969.

Sue, Derald Wing. *Microaggressions and Marginality: Manifestation, Dynamics, and Impact.* New York: Wiley, 2010.

Svendsen, Adam. "The Globalization of Intelligence since 9/11: Frameworks and Operational Parameters." *Cambridge Review of International Affairs* 21, no. 1 (2008): 129–44.

Taylor, Phillip. "Weapons Standardization in NATO: Collaborative Security or Economic Competition?" *International Organization* 36, no. 1 (1982): 95–112.

Thrift, Nigel, and Andrew Leyshon. "A Phantom State? The De-Traditionalization of Money, the International Financial System and International Financial Centres." *Political Geography* 13, no. 4 (1994): 299–327.

U.S. Congress. NATO *Standardization, Interoperability and Readiness: Report of the Special Subcommittee on* NATO *Standardization, Interoperability, and Readiness of the Committee on Armed Services, House of Representatives.* Washington: U.S. Government Printing Office, 1979.

Vanhoonacker, Sophie, and Karolina Pomorska. "The European External Action Service and Agenda-Setting in European Foreign Policy." *Journal of European Public Policy* 20, no. 9 (2013): 1316–31.

Vincent, Andrew. *Theories of the State.* New York: Wiley-Blackwell, 1991.

Vucetic, Srdjan. *The Anglosphere: A Genealogy of a Racialized Identity in International Relations.* Stanford: Stanford University Press, 2011.

———. "Bound to Follow? The Anglosphere and U.S.-Led Coalitions of the Willing, 1950–2001." *European Journal of International Relations* 17, no. 1 (2011): 27–49.

Walker, R. B. J. *Inside/Outside: International Relations as Political Theory.* Cambridge: Cambridge University Press, 1993.

Wallander, Celeste. "Institutional Assets and Adaptability: NATO after the Cold War." *International Organization* 54, no. 4 (2000): 705–35.

Warf, Barney. *Time-Space Compression: Historical Geographies.* London: Routledge, 2008.

Weisser, Florian. "Practices, Politics, Performativities: Documents in the International Negotiations on Climate Change." *Political Geography* 40, nos. A1–A2 (2014): 46–55.

Westerfield, H. Bradford. "America and the World of Intelligence Liaison." *Intelligence and National Security* 11, no. 3 (1996): 523–60.

Wieland, Christian. "The Consequences of Early Modern Diplomacy: Entanglement, Discrimination, Mutual Ignorance—and State Building." *Structures on the Move: Technologies of Governance in Transcultural Encounter,* ed. Antje Flüchter and Susann Richter, 271–84. Heidelberg: Springer Science and Business Media, 2012.

Williams, Paul. "Who's Making UK Foreign Policy?" *International Affairs* 80, no. 5 (2004): 909–29.

Woodward, Keith. "Affect, State Theory, and the Politics of Confusion." *Political Geography* 41, no. 1 (2014): 21–31.

Committee for Standardization (NATO), 79, 90
Common Agricultural Policy, 105
commonality, 85, 135
Common Foreign and Security Policy, 20, 99, 101, 105, 109, 124–25
Commonwealth, 58, 68, 74
Commonwealth Relations Office, 30
Communications Branch (National Research Council), 68
Communications-Electronics Coordination Section, 79
comparative trials, 90–92
compatibility, 85, 135
Conference of National Armaments Directors (CNAD), 92–93
Conference on Security and Cooperation in Europe. *See* Organization for Security and Cooperation in Europe
Congress of Vienna, 13–14
Coreu, 108–9, 124, 127, 131
CREAM, 55–56, 126
Crimean War, 28, 47

Daniel Report, 94–95, 130
database, 84–85
Defence Signals Branch, 68
de Gaulle, Charles, 102, 117, 126
DeLanda, Manuel, 10–11, 15
Dickens, Charles, 1–2
diplomacy, 3, 12–13, 44, 78, 81, 100, 120, 124, 128, 133, 136; diplomatico-military dispositif, 12, 31; diplomatic practices, 7, 123; diplomatic system, 11, 25–29, 31–32, 44, 137; embassies, 61
Douglas-Home, Sir Alec, 119

E-3A Airborne Early Warning and Control System, 86
ECHELON, 63
ECHO, 109–10
ECM Mark II device, 59
efficiency, 39–42, 44–45, 139
EGOTISTICAL GIRAFFE, 62
Eisenhower, Dwight, 73, 125
Élysée Treaty, 115
encryption, 43, 51, 65, 130, 139
Europe, 3, 12, 123

European Community. *See* European Union
European correspondent, 113–14, 136
European Union, 18, 99, 101–2, 104–6, 123; Commission, 23, 101, 106, 109, 111, 133; Council of Ministers, 99, 100, 102–4, 106, 111, 114–15, 118–19, 131; Europeanization, 114; European Quarter, 99, 110; External Action Service, 23, 99, 100, 101, 106–11, 114, 118–20, 133, 138–39; Parliament, 133; political cooperation, 102–6, 113, 125, 133

Falkland Islands War, 65
fiber-optic cables, 61–62
FN rifle, 75, 88
force relations, 8–9, 15, 27, 76, 128
Foreign Affairs Council. *See* European Union: Council of Ministers
Foreign and Commonwealth Office, 25, 30, 45–48, 114–15, 117–20, 132; building on Downing Street, 26–28, 32, 36–38, 41–47, 137; building on Whitehall, 29, 45, 127, 130–31, 138; Foreign Office (pre-FCO), 19, 23–26, 30–33, 39–43, 68, 74, 88, 124, 129, 132, 137–39
Foucault, Michel, 5, 11–13, 39

Gothic design, 43–44
governmentality, 11, 14, 30–31, 45, 87, 137
Government Code & Cipher School (GC&CS), 50, 55, 66
Government Communications Headquarters (GCHQ), 50, 57, 62, 64–68
Group of Four, 93

Habitus, 8
Hammond, Edmund, 33, 40–42, 132
Hanslope Park, 30, 46
harmonization, 14, 55, 76–78, 84, 88, 102, 116, 125, 134–36
hegemony, 96, 124
Hertslet, Lewis, 33, 36
hierarchy, 86–87, 106, 121, 132–34
High Representative for CFSP, 105–6, 117–18
Home Office, 26, 29–30
Horse Guards Parade, 44